DISEASES & DISORDERS

Blindness

Hal Marcovitz

LUCENT BOOKS
A part of Gale, Cengage Learning

GALE
CENGAGE Learning·

Detroit • New York • San Francisco • New Haven, Conn • Waterville, Maine • London

LIBRARY OF CONGRESS CATALOGING-IN-PUBLICATION DATA

Marcovitz, Hal.
 Blindness / By Hal Marcovitz.
  p. cm. — (Diseases & disorders)
 Includes bibliographical references and index.
 ISBN 978-1-4205-0041-7 (hardcover)
 1. Blindness—Juvenile literature. I. Title.
 RE91.M36 2009
 617.7'12—dc22

                                        2008016447

Lucent Books
27500 Drake Rd.
Farmington Hills, MI 48331

ISBN-13: 978-1-4205-0041-7
ISBN-10: 1-4205-0041-4

Table of Contents

"The Most Difficult Puzzles Ever Devised"

Charles Best, one of the pioneers in the search for a cure for diabetes, once explained what it is about medical research that intrigued him so. "It's not just the gratification of knowing one is helping people," he confided, "although that probably is a more heroic and selfless motivation. Those feelings may enter in, but truly, what I find best is the feeling of going toe to toe with nature, of trying to solve the most difficult puzzles ever devised. The answers are there somewhere, those keys that will solve the puzzle and make the patient well. But how will those keys be found?"

Since the dawn of civilization, nothing has so puzzled people—and often frightened them, as well—as the onset of illness in a body or mind that had seemed healthy before. A seizure, the inability of a heart to pump, the sudden deterioration of muscle tone in a small child—being unable to reverse such conditions or even to understand why they occur was unspeakably frustrating to healers. Even before there were names for such conditions, even before they were understood at all, each was a reminder of how complex the human body was, and how vulnerable.

While our grappling with understanding diseases has been frustrating at times, it has also provided some of humankind's most heroic accomplishments. Alexander Fleming's accidental discovery in 1928 of a mold that could be turned into penicillin has resulted in the saving of untold millions of lives. The isolation of the enzyme insulin has reversed what was once a death sentence for anyone with diabetes. There have been great strides in combating conditions for which there is not yet a cure, too. Medicines can help AIDS patients live longer, diagnostic tools such as mammography and ultrasounds can help doctors find tumors while they are treatable, and laser surgery techniques have made the most intricate, minute operations routine.

This "toe-to-toe" competition with diseases and disorders is even more remarkable when seen in a historical continuum. An astonishing amount of progress has been made in a very short time. Just two hundred years ago, the existence of germs as a cause of some diseases was unknown. In fact, it was less than 150 years ago that a British surgeon named Joseph Lister had difficulty persuading his fellow doctors that washing their hands before delivering a baby might increase the chances of a healthy delivery (especially if they had just attended to a diseased patient)!

Each book in Lucent's Diseases and Disorders series explores a disease or disorder and the knowledge that has been accumulated (or discarded) by doctors through the years. Each book also examines the tools used for pinpointing a diagnosis, as well as the various means that are used to treat or cure a disease. Finally, new ideas are presented—techniques or medicines that may be on the horizon.

Frustration and disappointment are still part of medicine, for not every disease or condition can be cured or prevented. But the limitations of knowledge are being pushed outward constantly; the "most difficult puzzles ever devised" are finding challengers every day.

Who Are the Blind?

Blindness is a disability that afflicts more than 1 million Americans who fit the description of severe vision impairment. Although many of them do not live in total darkness, they cannot see an object clearly at a distance of 20 feet (6m) that a person with normal vision can see at 200 feet (60m). Therefore, they suffer from 20/200 vision. (Normal vision is defined as 20/20.) Another 12 million Americans suffer lesser degrees of vision impairment, which means that even with eyeglasses, they experience challenges in their daily lives.

Some blind people lost their sight at birth or soon after they were born. They suffered childhood diseases or perhaps they lost their vision in accidents or other mishaps. In their cases, blindness has robbed them of ever enjoying a memorable vision. As such, they spend their whole lives wondering what a blue sky may look like, how their brothers and sisters may appear, what the stars look like when they twinkle, or how a flower grows. The list of things they have never seen is endless.

Other blind people have lost their sight after years of being able to see, often as a result of disease. Increasingly, these people are adults in their forties, fifties, and sixties who develop eye diseases and blindness because of poor lifestyle choices—obesity, smoking, and alcohol use are all regarded as factors that contribute to eye disease. According to H. Dunbar Hoskins Jr., executive vice president of the American Academy of Ophthalmology, "The stark reality is that millions of people will suffer significant vision loss and blindness because they don't know the risks."[1] In fact, studies show that half of all Americans will experience some degree of eye disease as they grow older, and that the incidence of age-related eye disease in America will grow by 65 percent by the year 2020.

Global Concerns

On a global scale, the problem could be even more severe. According to the World Health Organization (WHO), the public health arm of the United Nations, as many as 300 million people will suffer from blindness or other severe vision disabilities by the year 2020—a rate that is double the current level. Part of the problem can be attributed to the aging populations of industrialized nations like the United States. In the United States, members of the so-called baby boom generation—the generation of Americans born in the twenty-year period following World War II—are now reaching their forties, fifties, and sixties and are starting to experience the effects of advancing age, including the loss of eyesight.

But the problem is also due to the continuing inability to deliver adequate health care to developing nations in Africa, Asia, Central America, South America, and other depressed regions of the planet. In developing countries, such preventable eye diseases as trachoma, which is a disease caused by a bacterial infection; xerophthalmia, blindness caused by a deficiency of vitamin A in the diet; and onchocerciasis, which is also known as river blindness and is caused by a parasitic worm, continue to afflict people who have few defenses against the ailments. The *UN Chronicle*, the official publication of the United Nations, reports:

> WHO experts say that more than two thirds of this blindness and visual disability could be avoided through adequate and timely prevention or treatment. At present, approximately 7 million people become blind each year. Over 70 percent of these people receive treatment and their vision is restored. Thus, the number of blind persons worldwide is currently increasing by up to 2 million per year.[2]

Diseases such as trachoma, xerophthalmia, and onchocerciasis are rare in the United States and other industrialized nations; nevertheless, blindness is hardly a rare condition. Indeed, most Americans have encountered blind people from time to time. They may be led by guide dogs, or they may carry white canes that they wave from side to side, searching for obstacles in their paths. In many cases, the tools they use—such as their white canes, guide dogs, or books in braille—are the only indication that they are vision impaired.

Today most blind people live full lives. Through the help of advocacy groups such as the National Federation of the Blind as well as laws that have helped preserve their rights, blind people have been able to free themselves from lives of poverty and menial labor to become contributing members of society. They work as professionals, marry and raise families, and enjoy their leisure time with friends. Blind people can often be seen riding buses or subways on their way to work, enjoying a beverage at a coffee bar, or waterskiing and snowboarding, albeit with the help of a guide. Many blind people go on to be-

An African man afflicted by river blindness checks his laundry. River blindness is common in Third World countries.

come leaders and trailblazers, such as Marla Runyan, a track star who, in 2000, became the first blind athlete to compete at the Olympics; and David Blunkett, one of Great Britain's most influential political leaders.

Stacy Cervenka, a congressional aide in Washington, D.C., was born with severe damage to her optical nerves. Her disability did not get in the way of forging a productive career and life. Following her graduation from college, Cervenka found a job on Capitol Hill. Even though she is blind and must walk with the aid of a white cane, Cervenka has learned her way around the Capitol so well that she is often called on to lead tours. She has compensated for her lack of vision by accessing computer software that provides audio descriptions of the Capitol architecture and by following other tour guides, committing to memory the route through the corridors of the Capitol.

During her leisure hours Cervenka enjoys the active lifestyle of a young woman on the go. "When I'm not working," she says, "I love to roller-blade, swim, read, watch movies, and travel. I also love to go dancing. I'm currently taking a pilates class, and I'm very active in my church. My goal is to do public policy in the field of education. I also hope to one day run for office myself."[3]

CHAPTER ONE

What Causes Blindness?

There are a dozen or more diseases of the eyes that can lead to a loss of sight, but the most prevalent are glaucoma, cataracts, age-related macular degeneration, and diabetic retinopathy. In most cases there are no cures for the diseases that cause blindness, although drugs can often ease the symptoms, and surgery may correct the damage.

Saddest, perhaps, are the diseases that afflict young children in the United States and elsewhere that leave them blind from birth or from very early ages. For example, babies born to pregnant women infected with syphilis or German measles may be born blind or lose their vision soon after birth. In other cases, mothers who do not practice proper prenatal care—they may abuse alcohol or drugs during their pregnancies—can place their babies' eyesight at risk.

Blindness can also be caused by diseases that do not specifically infect the eyes, such as meningitis and leprosy. Another cause of blindness can be trauma to the head or eyes: Victims of accidents, violence, or combat wounds often suffer loss of eyesight. The eyes are among the body's most fragile organs. When the eyes are exposed to disease or trauma, they may suffer long-lasting and irreversible damage that can result in disabilities lasting a lifetime.

Sharp Focus

Everybody is born with two eyes; they work in concert, act-ing as cameras that project three-dimensional images that are interpreted by the brain. The most obvious part of the eye is the "white" of the eye, which is known as the sclera. This is a tough, leathery outer coating that protects the delicate inte-rior parts of the eye. Another obvious feature of the eye is the iris, which gives the eye its color. The color of a person's eye depends on the amount of pigment, known as melanin, that is found in the eye tissue—the more pigment, the darker the iris. People with brown eyes have a lot of pigment in their eyes; people with blue eyes have less.

The iris has a function other than just giving somebody blue or brown eyes. The iris contains muscles that adjust the size of the pupil, which is the dark spot at the center of the iris. The pupil is simply a hole that opens and closes according to the amount of light that strikes the eye. On a bright day, the iris will close the pupil down to a very tiny opening, blocking most of the light. At night, the pupil will open wide. Covering the pupil, jutting out in a bulge from the sclera, is a layer of clear tissue known as the cornea. The cornea, shaped like a dome, bends the light that strikes the eye, directing it onto a lens found just behind the pupil.

The lens is made of transparent tissue. It is flexible and focuses by contracting and expanding. When an object is far away, the lens relaxes and grows thin. When an object is close, the lens compresses itself into a ball-like shape. This process is known as accommodation. Working together, the cornea and lens allow the eye to bring objects into sharp focus. Yet as the body ages, the lens loses its elasticity, making focusing difficult. That is why many people tend to need glasses as they grow older.

Behind the lens is a globelike space that composes most of the eye. This part of the eye is known as the vitreous cavity and is filled with a clear, jellylike substance known as vitreous humor. The vitreous cavity and its contents give the eye its shape and keep it from collapsing, much the way pressurized

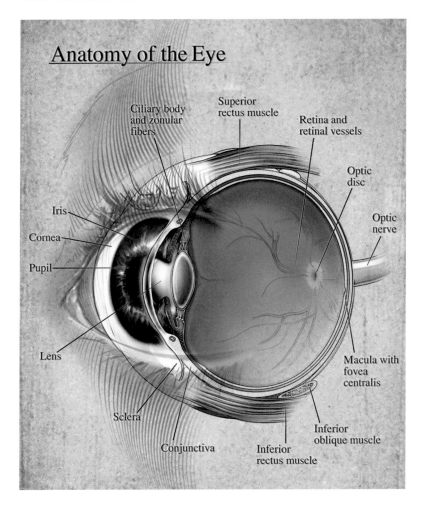

Anatomy of the Eye

Ciliary body and zonular fibers

Superior rectus muscle

Retina and retinal vessels

Optic disc

Optic nerve

Iris

Cornea

Pupil

Lens

Sclera

Conjunctiva

Inferior rectus muscle

Inferior oblique muscle

Macula with fovea centralis

air gives a basketball its shape. Also, the images projected by the lens pass through the vitreous cavity, meaning the fluid must be clear.

Rods and Cones

At the rear of the vitreous cavity, lining the back wall of the eye, is the retina. The retina contains millions of light-sensitive cells that capture the light projected by the lens. The cells are found in the shape of rods and cones. Rod cells absorb dim light and enhance peripheral vision by capturing images along the sides of the eyes. Cone cells absorb images that are straight ahead, containing a lot of detail. The cone cells also capture brighter lights and distinguish colors. That is why it is often difficult to make out colors at night—the rod cells, which do not distinguish colors, are doing most of the work.

At the center of the retina is the macula, which is densely packed with cone cells. The macula is important for reading and doing other things up close, such as threading a needle.

The information projected by the cornea, focused by the lens, and gathered by the retina is carried to the brain by a bundle of more than a million nerve fibers. This bundle is known as the optic nerve, which transmits the information to the brain through a process that involves chemical reactions and electrical impulses. The brain then digests the information and produces an image of what the eyes see.

There are many other parts of the eye, including blood vessels that provide nutrients to the eye, tiny fibers that hold the lens in place, and a muscle known as the choroid that rests between the retina and inner layer of the sclera. All these parts serve important functions and must work together in order for the eye to function properly.

Fuzzy Vision

Of course, all these parts often do not function properly, which is why many people wear glasses. When the cornea and lens focus light in front of the retina, a person is nearsighted, meaning things at a distance appear fuzzy. When the light hits the retina before it is focused, a person is farsighted, meaning he or she may have trouble reading or seeing things clearly up close. Just being nearsighted or farsighted does not mean somebody has a disease of the eyes and is in danger of losing sight. Most cases of nearsightedness, farsightedness, and other common vision defects are correctable with glasses.

Still, fuzzy vision may be an early symptom of eye disease. The most widespread disease that affects the eye is cataracts, which afflict more than 20 million Americans, most over age forty. A cataract is a cloud that forms on the lens. In Latin, *cataracta* means "waterfall," meaning that living with a cataract is like trying to see through a waterfall. Most cataracts are caused by aging—eyes develop cloudy lenses just as hair sometimes turns gray. In the eye, the lens is composed of water and fibers of protein; when the fibers age, they often deteriorate. A cataract is a deterioration of the protein fibers in the lens of the eye. As the cataract grows worse, it may turn the lens yellow, green, or brown. This type of cataract is known as a nuclear cataract.

Other types of cataracts include cortical and subcapsular cataracts. A cortical cataract is composed of whitish, wedge-shaped streaks that form on the edge of the lens. As the cataract grows worse, the streaks extend to the center of the lens. People with cortical cataracts have trouble focusing their eyes and are bothered by glare and bright lights. A subcapsular cataract forms at the back of the lens. It manifests itself in a small dark spot that blocks the light passing through the lens on the way to the retina. People with cortical cataracts have trouble reading and are bothered by bright lights. Often somebody with a cortical cataract will see the glow of a halo around a bright light.

A cloudy lens of an eye with a cataract is contrasted with a normal, healthy lens.

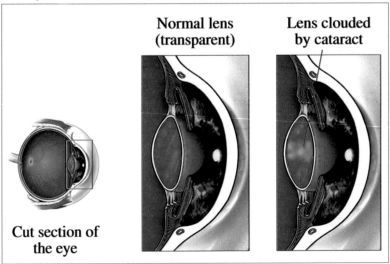

Normal lens (transparent)

Lens clouded by cataract

Cut section of the eye

Eventually, cataracts can lead to blindness. The disease is responsible for about half of all cases of blindness or severe vision impairment in the United States. Cataract damage can be repaired through surgery, however; about 1.5 million cataract surgeries occur each year, and most are performed on patients over the age of sixty-five. Physicians usually recommend surgery if the patient scores below 20/50 on a vision test. In cataract surgery, doctors can often wipe out the fuzzy patches or streaks with laser technology. In a newer procedure, physicians can wipe the lenses clean by blasting the cataracts with ultrasound waves. The procedure can be performed in less than thirty minutes in a doctor's office. Also, the surgery has proven to be very successful—about 98 percent of the patients receive relief from their cataracts. In more severe cases, though, a much more invasive operation may be recommended. In such cases, the damaged lens is removed and replaced with an artificial lens.

A Buildup of Pressure

Glaucoma is another disease that mostly affects older adults; more than 2.2 million Americans suffer from the affliction. Glaucoma is a buildup of pressure in the eye that eventually damages the optic nerve. The eye is constantly manufacturing new vitreous humor and draining old fluid through a system of ducts between the iris and cornea known as the trabecular network. If the ducts are blocked, the old fluid cannot drain, causing increased pressure inside the vitreous cavity. It is as though too much air has been pumped into a basketball. In its later stages, glaucoma can be painful, causing headaches and pain in the eyes as well as blurred vision.

People can live with glaucoma for years without knowing they have it. Eventually, though, they may notice their lack of peripheral vision—the ability to see things that are not directly in front of them. They also have trouble seeing at night and differentiating between light and dark shades. In addition, their eyes grow sensitive to bright lights and glare. Their vision will grow worse as their optic nerves deteriorate further; eventually, they can go blind.

Hallucinations and Vision Loss

People who suffer from severe vision loss often develop Charles Bonnet syndrome, which causes them to hallucinate. The condition is named after an eighteenth-century Swiss scientist who first reported the syndrome in his eighty-seven-year-old grandfather.

Research shows that as many as 15 percent of people whose vision is worse than 20/60 have hallucinated. In fact, it may be even more prevalent because people who hallucinate do not like to admit to it, fearing that they would be regarded as mentally ill.

"It is not a rare disorder," says V.S. Ramachandran, a physician at the University of California at San Diego who has studied the syndrome. "It's quite common. It's just that people don't want to talk about it when they have it."

Patients who have talked about their hallucinations say the images vary and have included illustrations of geometric patterns, images of landscapes or people, or fantastic shapes and characters straight out of science-fiction movies. One patient, retired San Diego schoolteacher Nancy Johnson, who lost an eye to cancer, says, "I see little tiny geometric shapes that fit together, like doodles in the margin of a notebook. It's sort of interesting and distracting, but it's not fearful."

Quoted in Susan Kruglinski, "When the Vision Goes, the Hallucinations Begin," *New York Times*, September 14, 2004.

Charles Bonnet, shown here, noticed his grandfather's hallucinatory symptoms as his eyesight worsened.

Glaucoma may be genetic in origin; there is often a family history of the disease. Also, it can develop simply because some people's eyes grow into a shape that limits drainage through the trabecular network. In some people, their lenses grow larger as they age, which pushes the iris against the cornea, narrowing the escape route for the vitreous humor.

Glaucoma can lead to blindness if the optic nerve is damaged by the pressure. There is no cure for glaucoma, but the disease responds to drug therapy. Physicians can administer drugs, either orally or through eye drops, that ease the pressure in the eyes. New surgical techniques, often involving lasers, can be used to ease the symptoms as well. One form of laser surgery can cut away part of the trabecular network, which causes remaining parts of the network to stretch wider, enabling the vitreous humor to drain. Conventional surgery may also be employed to cut openings into the trabecular network.

Deterioration of the Macula

Age-related macular degeneration (AMD) is yet another eye disease that is most common in older adults, with some 1.7 million sufferers in the United States. As the name suggests, the disease causes the deterioration of the macula. Symptoms include blurred vision and blind spots in the center of the field of view. Reading may become more difficult. Also, straight lines—such as those painted down the middle of a road—often appear crooked to an AMD patient.

AMD does not cause total blindness. The disease affects only the field of view that is directly ahead; therefore, sufferers of macular degeneration retain their peripheral vision. Nevertheless, AMD can have a dramatic effect on the ability to read or perform simple tasks, such as cooking a meal or finding something that has been dropped on the floor, because there always seems to be a fuzzy cloud in the way.

There are two forms of AMD. Dry AMD progresses slowly, killing the cells in the macula over a period of years and forcing a gradual erosion in the ability to see. The dry form afflicts about 90 percent of AMD patients. The others are afflicted with wet AMD, which is a more severe form of the disease. In wet AMD, new but abnormal blood vessels grow beneath the retina. In most cases, the tiny and fragile vessels rupture and bleed, which kills the cells of the macula. Someone afflicted with wet AMD can suffer a rapid loss of vision, going nearly blind within a few days or weeks.

Dry AMD is caused by a breakdown in the ability of a waste disposal system in the eye to rid itself of dead macula cells. In the macula, new cells constantly replace old cells. If the eye is working properly, a layer of the retina known as the retinal pigment epithelium carries old cells away, depositing them in the choroid. As people grow older, the eye's ability to dispose of these cells decreases, which means the old cells are left behind, where they clog up the macula and enhance its deterioration. In wet AMD, when the rogue blood vessels rupture, they leave behind scar tissue that forms on the macula, causing a permanent blockage in vision.

Fred Lopez, a former attorney for the U.S. Bureau of Alcohol, Tobacco, and Firearms in Berkeley, California, developed wet AMD. He recalls learning, quite suddenly, that his vision was deteriorating. It happened on a sunny day as he walked to his car. As he passed a sign, he discovered he could not read it. "It was just blurry and out of focus,"[4] he says.

There is no cure for dry AMD. Dry AMD sufferers can only adjust to their lives and hope the disease progresses slowly. There is not much hope for wet AMD patients, either. Laser surgery can seal the rogue blood vessels, but the damage that has already been done is irreversible. One wet AMD patient, Lloyd Barnard, a retired mechanical engineer from Atlanta, Georgia, has learned to live with the disability. He uses large magnifying glasses to read. "I have learned to enjoy each day and to see a lot more with my mind,"[5] he says.

Complications of Diabetes

One of the few eye diseases that targets young adults is diabetic retinopathy, which is a complication of diabetes

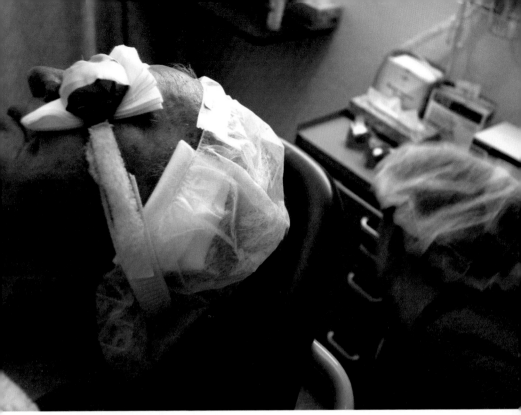

An AMD patient rests after undergoing implantation of a tiny telescope as part of a clinical trial.

and is known to affect people as young as age twenty-five. About 4 million people suffer from the disease in the United States. In diabetic retinopathy, diabetes attacks the tiny blood vessels that nourish the retina. Typically, the vessels deteriorate because of the high levels of blood sugar common in diabetics.

There are two forms of the disease: nonproliferative diabetic retinopathy (NPDR) and proliferative diabetic retinopathy (PDR). In NPDR, the walls of the blood vessels in the retina weaken, forming tiny bulges that may rupture, causing blood and fluid to leak into the retina. Sufferers of NPDR endure fuzzy splotches blocking their vision. Also, in NPDR, the vessels in the macula may swell, causing a loss of direct vision, although as in AMD, peripheral vision is unaffected.

PDR is the more advanced form of the disease. In PDR, rogue blood vessels grow in the retina as well as the vitreous humor. These vessels may also bulge and leak blood, clouding the path of light from the lens to the retina. In severe cases, the vitreous cavity may fill with blood. Also, scar tissue may form on the retina, causing it to detach from the back of the eye.

People who suffer from diabetic retinopathy start seeing hazy specks, known as floaters, across their field of view. They will also soon see dark streaks or a red film clouding their vision. Blurred vision, poor night vision, difficulty adjusting from

A special microscopic image from an ophthalmoscope displays acute nonproliferative diabetic retinopathy.

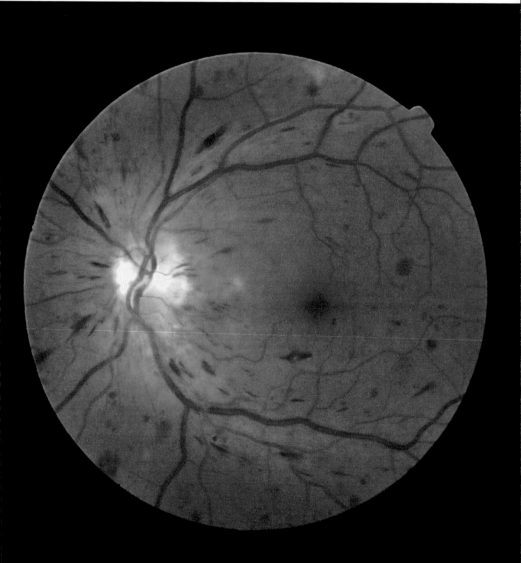

light to dark, and a dark spot in their direct vision is also common among sufferers of diabetic retinopathy.

The condition is caused by the high levels of blood sugar in the body, which eat away at the delicate walls of the blood vessels in the eyes. Blindness occurs when the vessels shut down, depriving the retina of oxygen. It is believed that most diabetics will eventually suffer some form of diabetic retinopathy, with many losing their eyesight. Diabetics can minimize the effects of the disease by closely monitoring their blood sugar levels; avoiding a high-fat diet, which contributes to diabetes; and maintaining normal blood pressure, which would put less stress on blood vessels.

Diabetic retinopathy is treated by laser surgery, which can seal leaky blood vessels. In cases where the vitreous cavity has filled with blood, a surgeon can repair the damaged vessels and then remove the vitreous humor. Next, the surgeon can fill the eye with a salt solution to maintain pressure inside the eye until the eye manufactures new vitreous humor. If the retina has become detached, this procedure may enable the retina to settle back into its place against the back wall of the eye.

Diseases That Afflict the Young

Cataracts, glaucoma, age-related macular degeneration, and diabetic retinopathy are diseases that affect mostly adults, but many young people lose their sight as well. When pregnant women contract syphilis or German measles, which is also known as rubella, the eyesight of their babies may be affected. Syphilis, a sexually transmitted disease, is spread by bacteria. German measles is spread by a virus. Both diseases can attack the organs, including the eyes, and cause blindness.

Other diseases can cause blindness as well, including meningitis and leprosy. Meningitis can cause blood vessels to leak, starving the body's organs, including the eyes, of blood. Leprosy, which is spread by bacteria, causes nerve and tissue damage and often affects the eyes. These diseases may be rare in the United States and other industrialized nations,

What Is Tunnel Vision?

Patients who suffer from the disease known as retinitis pigmentosa (RP) experience a degeneration of the rod cells in their eyes, which enable people to see in dark conditions. As such, RP patients often suffer from "night blindness"—they are unable to see clearly at night or in dark places, such as theaters.

As more rod cells are destroyed, RP patients lose their peripheral vision as well. As the disease grows worse, their eyesight deteriorates until their vision is limited to a very small circle of clarity that is directly in front of them. People with RP view the world as though they are looking out from the inside of a tunnel. RP can also spread to the cone cells, resulting in a complete loss of sight.

About one hundred thousand people suffer from RP in the United States. RP is an inherited disease, passed down through families. Little is known about what causes RP or what steps people can take to avoid the disease. Research has indicated, though, that RP can be slowed by increasing the amount of vitamin A in the diet. Vitamin A has been found to enhance the creation of rhodopsin, a protein that helps develop rod cells in the eye.

but in developing countries in Africa and Asia they can be common. There are other causes of blindness common in developing countries as well, including malnutrition, which results in a vitamin A deficiency in the body. Vitamin A is an important ingredient of the proteins that make up eye tissue.

The most common cause of blindness in a young child is retinopathy of prematurity (ROP), which is a scarring of the baby's retina due to improper development of blood vessels in the fetus. Children who are born very prematurely or have low birth weights—due mainly to poor diet or drug and alcohol abuse by their mothers—are very susceptible to ROP.

The genetic condition known as albinism may lead to severe vision problems in young children. Albinism manifests itself in a decreased amount of pigmentation in the skin, hair, and eyes. Children who are afflicted with albinism have very little melanin in their eyes; therefore, their eyes have little protection against sunlight. It may be very difficult for them to see in bright sunlight.

Other causes of blindness in young children are hydrocephalus, a condition in which there is an overabundance of fluid in the brain; congenital cytomegalovirus, a viral infection that afflicts the fetus; and birth asphyxia, a lack of oxygen to the baby during delivery. All of these afflictions attack organs in the baby's body, including the child's very sensitive eyes.

Combat Injuries

There are also nonmedical causes of blindness, including trauma to the eyes and head, such as automobile accidents and other mishaps and injuries suffered in combat. In fact, eye

Most Common Eye Diseases in Adult Americans

Eye Disease	Symptoms	Number of Americans
Cataracts	Fuzzy or cloudy vision; cloudy lens	20 million over age 40
Glaucoma	Headaches; eye pain; blurred vision	2.2 million
Age-related macular degeneration	Blurred vision; blind spots in the field of vision	1.7 million
Diabetic retinopathy	Floaters; cloudy vision; blurred vision; poor night vision; problems adjusting from light to dark; dark spot in the direct field of vision	4 million

injuries have surfaced as a major affliction affecting American military personnel serving in Afghanistan and Iraq. Since the two wars erupted, more than eleven hundred American troops have sustained injuries to their eyes, constituting 13 percent of all serious wounds suffered in the two wars.

Military experts believe the nature of the warfare in Iraq and Afghanistan may be the cause. Many American troops are injured by roadside bombs and mortar and grenade attacks, which send pieces of shrapnel flying in all directions. One such victim is Ivan Castro, an Army infantry officer from North Carolina who lost his vision when a mortar round struck a few feet from where he was perched atop a rooftop in Baghdad, damaging his eyes with flying shrapnel. Two of his companions were killed in the attack. "I was fortunate to make it," Castro says. "I had several injuries, definitely my blindness was the most severe, but I was on that line teetering between being here and being six feet under."[6]

Castro has entered a program that is helping him learn how to adjust to life without the use of his eyes. Barring new and dramatic advances in medical science, the damage to his eyes is probably irreversible. In fact, most people who lose their sight find themselves facing the truth that the condition of blindness is likely to stay with them for the rest of their lives.

CHAPTER TWO

The Long Road to Equality

Throughout history blind people have often been regarded as outcasts. They were left to beg in the streets during the Middle Ages and were warehoused in almshouses or institutions through the nineteenth century. It took until the closing years of the twentieth century before they finally won the right to be regarded as the equals of sighted people.

Nevertheless, throughout their struggle there has been no denying the talents of blind people. Over the years many have achieved tremendous accomplishments. The work of the ancient Greek poet Homer has endured for centuries. John Milton is one of England's greatest poets. American author and activist Helen Keller convinced generations of disabled people that they could not be held back by their handicaps. American recording artist Ray Charles may have been the twentieth century's most popular voice in rhythm and blues.

The accomplishments of Homer, Milton, Keller, and Charles show that blind people can go as far as their talents can take them. And yet, despite their accomplishments, there is no question that most blind people have struggled to prove themselves equal to persons of sight.

The Blind Bard

Homer, who lived during the eighth century B.C., is the author of two poems, the *Iliad* and the *Odyssey*, that have been read and studied for centuries. He is one of the most influential storytellers in history; his two epic poems relate the adventures of heroic figures. Little is known about the life of the ancient poet; indeed, for years, scholars have debated whether Homer was blind, with most concluding that as an adult Homer did lack eyesight. (In Greek, the word *homeros* can be interpreted to mean "blind.") In any event, the fact that Homer was blind did not detract from his ability to craft stories and develop fundamental literary themes of adventure and conquest that continue to be explored by authors and filmmakers centuries after his death.

Homer used his literature to explore blindness. In the *Odyssey*, Homer relates the story of Demodocus—the "blind bard"—who was robbed of his eyesight by a Muse, a daughter of the chief god Zeus. In return for his eyesight, the Muse gave Demodocus the power of song. According to Princeton University literature professor Robert Fagles, the story of Demodocus helped create the long-standing myth that blind people possess an insight into truth and beauty that sighted people lack—a concept that may have been embraced by readers of the *Iliad* and the *Odyssey*, who found it necessary to explain to themselves how a blind man could craft such gripping stories. As Fagles explains:

> The bard's reward for suffering blindness, the Muse might say, is his heightened power of insight. The artist who cannot see, in fact, must imagine—and finds the power to imagine—a poetic world that is more vivid, more compelling than any world which we might set our eyes on. That's the paradox of the blind bard, and perhaps of Homer himself, and why, in all probability, the legend of his blindness seems to last throughout the centuries.[7]

Over the centuries, other storytellers have treated blindness as a curse or source of evil. During the ancient era, it was believed that blind people were robbed of their vision as punishment for sin. Greek mythology relates the story of Phineus, who abused his gift of prophecy—the power of foresight—and was blinded by Zeus as punishment. Likewise, in the Greek

Homer, the ancient Greek poet, is widely believed to have been blind.

play *Oedipus at Colonus* by Sophocles, Oedipus blinds himself as punishment for killing his father and marrying his mother and then wanders aimlessly for the next twenty years. William Shakespeare also treated blindness as a punishment; in his tragedy *King Lear*, the character of the Earl of Gloucester has been blinded as punishment for committing adultery and then stumbles through life and is easily fooled by the lies of others.

Other authors have described blindness as a sign of evil. In *Treasure Island* by Robert Louis Stevenson, the wicked pirate Pew is blind, as is Stagg, a devious character in Charles Dickens's *Barnaby Rudge*. In *The Sea Wolf* by Jack London, Captain Wolf Larsen, one of American literature's most sinister characters, eventually loses his sight but still terrifies his crew. In J.R.R. Tolkien's *Lord of the Rings*, the evil spider Shelob manages to lure victims into her lair and consume them, even though she is blind.

The Yoke of Blindness

Although Homer's blindness has been debated by scholars, there has never been a question about the blindness that afflicted John Milton. Born in 1608, Milton started suffering from failing eyesight in his forties. Historians believe he suffered from glaucoma. By 1652 Milton was totally blind.

Milton was a prolific writer and political figure—he served for a time as British foreign secretary—but his greatest achievement as a poet came after he lost his eyesight. In 1667 he published *Paradise Lost*. This story of Satan's fall from heaven has established the eternal fight between good and evil as one of literature's most basic themes. Since he was blind, Milton was forced to dictate the poem to a stenographer.

Milton explored blindness in several of his works, particularly the poem "On His Blindness," which he wrote the year he lost his sight. In the poem Milton appeals to God, asking how he can serve the Lord without the use of vision. In his response, God admonishes Milton to be patient and bear the "yoke" of blindness. He also tells Milton that people who can endure their handicaps can serve the Lord in their own ways. The final

Writer John Milton probably lost his vision due to glaucoma. He is shown here dictating to his daughter.

and often-quoted line of the poem reads, "They also serve who only stand and wait."[8]

Some blind people were not satisfied with simply enduring blindness. Despite their loss of vision, they intended to live full and productive lives. History includes many accounts of blind people who emerged as leaders. One of the first was Hitoyasu, a ninth-century Japanese prince who served as a provincial governor despite the handicap of blindness. Another blind monarch was George Frederick, who ruled the region of Germany known as Hanover in the 1850s. During the fifteenth century, Bohemian general Johann Ziska led a force of forty thousand men against an invading Hungarian army. Ziska suffered the loss of an eye in an earlier battle; shortly before commencing the engagement against the Hungarians, the general lost the use of his other eye after sustaining a head wound.

Despite being totally blind, Ziska insisted on remaining at the head of his army. Accompanied during the battle by two cavalry soldiers who led his horse, Ziska orchestrated the attack, which resulted in a rout of the invading army.

Schools for the Blind

Homer, Milton, Ziska, and the others were unique figures in history; for most other blind people, the affliction of blindness meant a life of poverty and anguish. Most blind people were forced to beg in the streets. Indeed, for centuries society was slow to recognize the abilities of blind people to fend for themselves or provide them with education or laws guaranteeing their rights.

Few schools were established to teach blind people. In fact, society believed that blindness was due to mental frailty—the blind were incapable of learning, so why bother teaching them? Most homes for blind people were established by churches, which regarded them as outcasts and took them in as charity cases. These were mostly refuges such as almshouses, where blind people were provided with food, clothing, a place to sleep, and not much else. Some of these institutions were endowed with generous sums of money by kings and wealthy nobles who, as they grew older and neared death, opened their pocketbooks in the hopes that their charitable acts would be viewed with favor by the Almighty. Shortly before he died in 1087, the Norman king William the Conqueror endowed four homes for the blind in England, an appropriate act of charity given the fact that he often dealt with his enemies by gouging out their eyes.

As for teaching the blind, a few educators tried, but a major impediment to their efforts was always the question of how to teach the blind to read. One of the first to try was Girolamo Cardano, a sixteenth-century Italian mathematician who realized the blind could use the power of touch to understand the written word. He had letters of the alphabet engraved on sheets of metal and instructed his pupils to identify each character by using their fingers. Other teachers of the blind had the alphabet carved into planks of wood or fashioned into wax shapes. All of these efforts met with mixed degrees of success. Clearly, the lines, circles, and curlicues found in written script were too difficult for most blind people to follow.

The Royal Institute for Blind Youth

Eventually, though, innovators developed improvements, making it somewhat easier for blind people to read. In the seventeenth century a Catholic priest, Francesco Lana-Terzi (who also suggested that deaf people could understand speech by learning to read lips) had each letter of the alphabet fashioned within its own embossed block. That helped blind people determine where one letter ended and another began. Other innovators, who concluded that the letters themselves were

In 1876 Paris, young blind men play cards at the academy for the blind established by Valentin Haüy. The school was the first of its kind.

confusing the blind readers, substituted symbols or numerals for the characters of the alphabet.

Although blind readers were stumbling over the words on the embossed pages, there is no question that the education of blind people had progressed well beyond the days when they were locked away in almshouses. In the late eighteenth century, Frenchman Valentin Haüy established the first academy for the blind in Paris. Haüy started his school after watching a crowd mock four old blind men begging in the street. The men, dressed in outlandish robes and dunce caps, were hoping to attract alms by making noise on musical instruments. Saddened by what he witnessed, Haüy declared, "I will substitute the truth for this mocking parody. I will make the blind read! I will put in their hands volumes printed by themselves. They will trace the true characters and will read their own writing, and they shall be enabled to execute harmonious concerts."[9] He opened his school in 1784.

Two years later Haüy presented his twenty-four best pupils in the court of King Louis XVI, where they displayed their ability to read. (Haüy used a system that employed characters of the alphabet embossed into heavy sheets of paper.) Haüy's students could also write, perform mathematical computations, and play musical instruments. Awestruck by the demonstration, Louis and his queen, Marie Antoinette, provided Haüy's school with a generous endowment. In 1806 Haüy left the school, now known as the Royal Institute for Blind Youth, to establish similar academies in Germany and Russia.

Although Haüy had moved on, the school he established continued to be a leader in educating the blind. In 1819 Louis Braille enrolled as a student in the institute. Braille, ten years old when he arrived, had been blinded in an accident at the age of three. Braille proved to be something of a musical prodigy. He learned to play the organ, and at the age of sixteen he accepted a job as the organist for a church located near the institute.

At the age of nineteen, Braille was appointed to a teaching position at the institute. A year later he learned of a code developed by Charles Barbier, a French army captain. To keep mili-

This 1887 engraving shows the innovator Louis Braille, who created the braille system of reading and writing for the blind.

tary communications from falling into enemy hands, Barbier created a language consisting of twelve dots arranged in patterns. In addition, Barbier had the patterns embossed, so they could be read at night by touch—in fact, Barbier referred to his code as "night writing." The code was based on phonetics—the patterns did not stand for individual letters of the alphabet, but rather the sounds made by the letters.

Administrators of the institute thought the system could be employed to teach the blind to read, but the code proved to be too complicated for the students to follow. Braille, now just twenty years old, refined the code, reducing the number of dots from twelve to six. He also based the code on the alphabet rather than on phonetic sounds. In addition, he developed patterns to stand for punctuation as well as numerals and musical notes. Braille's system, soon to become known by the name of its creator, was eventually adopted by schools for the blind across the globe. Nearly two centuries after its creation, braille remains the most important tool that has been developed for the education of blind people.

The Miracle Worker

Haüy's influence spread across the Atlantic. In 1829 a Boston physician, John Dix Fisher, persuaded the Massachusetts legislature to establish a school for the blind. As a medical student, Fisher visited Paris and toured the Royal Institute. He returned to America with the resolve to establish a similar institution in the United States.

The first school for the blind in America opened in 1831 with seven students. Fisher's former college classmate, Samuel Gridley Howe—his wife, Julia Ward Howe, would later compose the lyrics for "The Battle Hymn of the Republic"—agreed to head the new school, to be known as the Massachusetts Asylum for the Blind. Later the institution was renamed the Perkins School for the Blind after a wealthy trustee, Thomas Perkins, donated his mansion to the school.

In 1880 fourteen-year-old Anne Sullivan enrolled as a student at the Perkins School. Sullivan was an orphan who lived in a Boston almshouse. She had been blinded by trachoma, but an operation restored partial vision. Sullivan graduated from Perkins in 1886; a year later, she was summoned to Tuscumbia, Alabama. A wealthy estate owner, Arthur H. Keller, had written to Perkins asking for a teacher who could work with his six-year-old daughter, Helen, who lost her vision and hearing as a baby after contracting what is believed to have been meningitis.

Anne Sullivan (right), reading a book aloud to her pupil Helen Keller, also finger spells the words. Sullivan taught Keller how to communicate.

The story of how Anne Sullivan led Helen Keller out of the darkness of her afflictions has served to inspire generations of handicapped people who, by Keller's example, learned that even the most debilitating of disabilities can be conquered. Unable to communicate with her student by spoken word, Sullivan taught Helen to read, speak, and communicate with others by a sign language known as finger spelling. On the day Sullivan arrived at the Keller home, she gave Helen a doll. Helen later wrote:

> When I played with it a little while, Miss Sullivan slowly spelled into my hand the word "d-o-l-l." I was at once interested in this finger play and tried to imitate it. When I finally succeeded in making the letters correctly I was flushed with childhood pleasure and pride. Running downstairs to my mother I held up my hand and made the letters for doll. I did not know that I was spelling a word or even that words existed; I was simply making my fingers go in monkey-like imitation. In the days that followed I learned to spell in this uncomprehending way a great many words, among them *pin, hat, cup* and a few verbs like *sit, stand* and *walk.* But my teacher had been with me several weeks before I understood that everything has a name.[10]

The little girl who had been living in virtual darkness eventually graduated from college and became an author and activist for the rights of women and disabled people. The story of Sullivan's relationship with Keller was later dramatized in a Broadway play and Academy Award–winning film titled *The Miracle Worker.*

Exploding into Stardom

Soon after the Perkins School opened its doors, schools for the blind were established in other American cities. A school in New York was established in 1832, followed two years later by a school in Philadelphia. In 1884 a state-sponsored school

Laura Bridgman

In 1837 Perkins School director Samuel Gridley Howe accepted seven-year-old Laura Bridgman as a student. At the age of two Laura had contracted scarlet fever, which robbed the young girl of her vision and hearing. By the time she entered Perkins, communication with Laura was mostly limited to pushing or pulling her in whatever direction she needed to go, and by showing approval by patting her on the head and disapproval by patting her back.

Braille had not yet been adopted by the Perkins School, but Howe managed to teach Laura to read by use of pages embossed with raised letters of the alphabet. Next, she learned sign language by finger spelling.

Laura's story eventually came to the attention of English author Charles Dickens, who met her during a visit to the school in 1842. Dickens wrote about Laura in his book *American Notes*. Years later the parents of Helen Keller read the book and contacted the Perkins School, hoping that the school could also teach their blind and deaf daughter to communicate. Anne Sullivan, a young teacher at the school, accepted the challenge and became Helen's teacher. During her years at Perkins, Sullivan was taught the techniques of finger spelling by Laura Bridgman.

for the blind and deaf opened in St. Augustine, Florida. In 1937 a blind seven-year-old boy named Ray Charles Robinson enrolled in the school.

The boy lost his sight to what is believed to have been a rare case of childhood glaucoma. Born into poverty in Albany, Georgia, Ray had been exposed to music at an early age by an elderly neighbor, who taught him to play the piano. When Ray entered the St. Augustine school, he was hardly an accomplished musician, but eight years later, when he left the school at the age of fifteen, he could play the piano, organ, alto

Blind musician Ray Charles plays chess using a special chessboard with niches in this 1966 photo.

saxophone, and other instruments as well. He also performed vocals and wrote music, including complicated arrangements for jazz and swing bands that employed sixteen or more instruments. He later recalled:

> While I was at the school, I formed a little group and we started out playing for ladies' tea parties and church socials on Sundays. That would bring in two or three bucks, which was pretty good wages for a young kid with no expenses. When I left the school, I decided that I'd just keep making music, instead of mops and brooms, which is what they taught us to do at school. I've never regretted it.[11]

In 1950 the young singer and songwriter settled in California, where his career was about to explode into stardom. By this time he had shortened his name to Ray Charles. By the 1960s Charles was among the most popular entertainers in the world. He churned out numerous hits, mostly in the genre of rhythm and blues, and won a dozen Grammy Awards.

Mostly, Charles never let his blindness get in the way of his life. He learned to play chess, keeping up with his opponent by feeling the pieces on the board. He enjoyed riding a motor scooter: Charles would take the scooter to a closed track and ride behind another scooter, following the sound of the engine ahead of him. He took flying lessons and often seized the controls of his private plane, albeit always with the pilot sitting alongside. One time Charles even fixed the engine of his airplane, finding and tightening a loose bolt by feel that the mechanic failed to see. Indeed, Charles once told an interviewer that he really did not miss his vision. He said:

> I can't say as I miss a hell of a lot. I don't care that much about driving a car. I've got a Cadillac and a Volkswagen, and to me, riding in one is about the same as riding in the

Picasso's Blue Period

For centuries blindness was perceived as either a punishment or a source of evil, and therefore it was to be feared. The Spanish artist Pablo Picasso is believed to have harbored a deep fear that he would one day lose his sight, particularly since his father's eyesight was failing. During Picasso's so-called Blue Period, the period from 1901 through 1904 in which he painted mostly in blue pigments, the artist rendered a number of images depicting blind people.

He often painted them as sad and lonely figures, a mood emphasized by his use of cold blue shades. Typical from this period was his 1904 painting *The Old Guitarist*, which depicts a thin and frail old blind man strumming a guitar. Other images from the Blue Period include *La Celestine*, a portrait of an elderly woman based on a one-eyed character featured in a fifteenth-century Spanish novel, and *The Blind Man's Meal*, in which Picasso depicts a gaunt blind man feeling along objects on a table for a jug of wine.

Clearly, Picasso was in a melancholy mood during the Blue Period, and he chose to illustrate his sadness by depicting images of blind people. In 1905 he met and fell in love with a young woman, Fernande Olivier, a liaison that prompted him to enter the Rose Period, in which he painted in warm red and pink shades, mostly depicting circus performers, clowns, and other lighthearted images.

other. I follow what's going on on television by the sound track, just like I do in real life. The same goes for the movies. . . . I get just as much from being around my kids, hearing them and touching them and looking into their insides, as most other parents, who can see. And I know my wife is a beautiful woman.[12]

Claiming Their Rights

Charles's rise to stardom occurred during an era in which African Americans and other minorities as well as women started winning rights that had been long denied to them. During the twentieth century blind people started agitating for their rights as well. They were helped by advocacy groups, mostly composed of leaders of the blind community. In 1921 the American Foundation for the Blind (AFB) was established, mostly to provide assistance to World War I veterans who lost their vision in the conflict. A similar group, the National Federation of the Blind (NFB), was established in 1940. The NFB, which adopted the slogan "Changing What It Means to Be Blind," sees its role as an advocacy group that presses for new laws that help blind people claim their rights.

Over the years the AFB, the NFB, and other advocacy groups have become influential organizations on behalf of blind people. Their efforts led to the establishment of the so-called white cane laws, which give blind pedestrians using canes or led by guide dogs the right of way at all intersections. Today all fifty states observe white cane laws.

Advocates for the blind also lobbied for passage of the Americans with Disabilities Act, the 1990 law that prohibits discrimination against handicapped people and requires public institutions to make buildings handicapped accessible. The act includes provisions for all handicapped people, such as curb cuts that make intersections accessible to wheelchairs and public bathrooms outfitted for disabled people. Some provisions of the act include specific provisions for blind people. For example, elevators in public buildings must include control buttons embossed with braille symbols.

Nevertheless, at the dawn of the twenty-first century, blind people in America and elsewhere continue to face many challenges as they exercise their rights and strive to achieve independence. As Kenneth Jernigan, the former president of the NFB, explains:

> Until only yesterday, blind people were completely excluded from the ranks of the normal community. In

early societies, they were reputedly abandoned, exter-
minated, or left to fend for themselves as beggars on
the lunatic fringe of the community. In the late Middle
Ages, so we are told, provision began to be made for
their care and protection in almshouses and other shel-
tered institutions. Only lately, it would seem, have blind
people begun stealthily to emerge from the shadows,
and to move in the direction of independence and self-
sufficiency.[13]

CHAPTER THREE

What Is Life Like for Blind People?

In 2006 a group of blind people brought a lawsuit against the federal government, alleging that the design of paper currency violates their rights since all denominations—ones, fives, tens, twenties, and so on—are the same size. U.S. district judge James Robertson agreed and issued an order directing the Treasury Department to redesign American currency so that blind people would be able to tell from the size of the bills, or from embossed symbols, the differences in denominations.

In making their case, attorneys for the blind plaintiffs argued that other countries have designed their currencies so blind people can tell the difference in the denominations by touch. In fact, one of the world's newest currencies—the Euro, which is used by most European countries—is issued in a different size for each denomination. "It's just frankly unfair that blind people should have to rely on the good faith of people they have never met in knowing whether they've been given the correct change,"[14] insisted Jeffrey A. Lovitky, an attorney who represents the blind plaintiffs.

Even so, a resolution to the issue may be years off. In late 2006 the federal government appealed Robertson's order, arguing that it would be too expensive to change the design of U.S.

currency. Government lawyers suggested it could cost more than $200 million to fashion new printing plates.

The reluctance of the federal government to make what would be a simple, albeit expensive, change in the design of American currency illustrates what it is like for a blind person in the United States as well as elsewhere in the world. Even the simple act of walking to the neighborhood diner for a cup of coffee requires planning, concentration, and the goodwill of others to ensure a safe and successful journey—and one that will not result in being cheated out of a few dollars in change by the cashier.

Thanks to his well-trained canine companion, a blind man is able to negotiate his neighborhood safely.

Guide Dogs

For a blind person, just taking a walk to the neighborhood diner can be an adventure. Many blind people rely on white canes and their memories. They have committed their routes to memory, counting the steps they must take to their destinations, where they must make turns, or where they will find steps and doors.

Many blind people rely on guide dogs. Worldwide there are more than seventy organizations that raise and train dogs to guide blind people. Using dogs as guides for the blind is a practice that dates back centuries—a Roman mural fashioned in the first century A.D. depicts a dog on a leash leading a blind man—but dogs were not trained specifically to assist blind people until World War I.

In Germany many soldiers returned from the war blinded by combat. In 1916 a German doctor, Gerhard Stalling, was examining patients in a military hospital when he was suddenly called away. Stalling left his dog in the care of a blind patient. When he returned to the man's bedside a short time later, he saw how well the patient and dog had bonded. Stalling established the first training center for guide dogs in the city of Oldenburg. Stalling's school soon opened branches in other cities, and by the end of the war the program was training six hundred dogs a year. In 1928 an American woman, Dorothy Eustis, established the Seeing Eye, the first program to train guide dogs in the United States.

Based in Morristown, New Jersey, the Seeing Eye is one of sixteen organizations in the United States that provide guide dogs to blind people. Other large groups include the Guide Dog Foundation in Smithtown, New York; Guide Dogs for the Blind in San Rafael, California; and Master Eye Foundation of Minneapolis, Minnesota.

It can cost as much as thirty-five thousand dollars to raise and train a guide dog. Most of the groups function as charities and charge blind people only nominal fees for the animals, if they charge anything at all. Typically, the groups recruit volunteers to raise and train the dogs. For example, under the direction of

Guide Dogs for the Blind, about one thousand puppies a year are raised by volunteers in eight Western states. Later the dogs work with their prospective blind partners, usually under the guidance of professional trainers.

Ignoring Distractions

Dogs are trained to be obedient, of course, but also to ignore distractions. Volunteers are encouraged to bring their dogs to work so that the animals can learn to be comfortable and quiet around many people. At Guide Dogs for the Blind, the final step in the dog's education is a twenty-five-day training session at the organization's headquarters, where the animal will be matched with a blind partner, who will then work closely with the dog until the two graduate from the program and return to the blind person's home.

A trained guide dog will learn the routine of its partner—the route he or she may walk to the bus, the grocery store, or the library. The dog will be trained to stop for steps, curbs, and other impediments. The dog will know not to lead its owner into traffic and to walk around obstacles, such as tree limbs, sign posts, and other pedestrians.

The animal and blind person must bond and learn to work as a team. John C. Ostiund, a Wyoming rancher who lost his sight at the age of fifty-seven due to diabetic retinopathy, says it took nearly a year before his guide dog, a black Labrador retriever named Jamie, learned his habits well enough to lead him through his daily life. "Had I been granted a magic carpet to take me where I wished, I could not have felt better than I did," Ostiund recalls. "The previous two years of shuffling along blindly, then with a white cane, had caused me to forget the barely discernible yet vivid pleasure of a swift walk by myself."[15]

Eventually Jamie learned the ranch so well that Ostiund need only tell the dog to lead him to the corral, barn, tack shed, or other places on the property. "For me," Ostiund says, "I began to feel there was hardly any limit to what I could do if I put my mind to it. What's more, we were having fun."[16]

A Labrador retriever puppy waits patiently for further instruction from his teacher. The dog is training to become a guide dog.

Still, dogs do not do everything for a blind person. A dog cannot count money for a blind person—as the federal lawsuit alleges, paper money does present its challenges. Until the federal government finds a way to make U.S. currency recognizable by its feel, many blind people will continue to rely on their own ways of folding currency—fives may be folded in half, twenties into quarters, and so on. Coins are easy to tell apart because they come in different sizes.

Seeing with One Hand

There is no question that a guide dog can be a valuable asset to a blind person whenever he or she takes a step out the front door. At home, though, blind people who live by themselves must be extremely self-reliant.

At home a blind person must be well organized. The furniture must be where he or she expects it to be, the box of cereal must be on the same kitchen shelf where it always is, the shirts must be put away in the same bureau drawer where the blind person expects to find them, and the toothbrush must be in its same location in the bathroom. Many blind people have created their own systems for helping themselves stay organized; they may take braille labels to stores with them and at checkout ask the baggers to place the labels on the groceries as they are placed into the bags.

Blind people can clean their own homes. They do it systematically, moving around each room in a clockwise direction, dusting from top to bottom. They usually do not have throw rugs in their homes—they are too easy to trip over— and they do not leave doors, drawers, or cabinet doors open. When pouring liquid from a bottle into a cup, a blind person will do it over the sink. Blind people use oven mitts instead of pot holders to take food out of the oven. Many of them squeeze toothpaste directly into their mouths or onto their fingers.

Author John M. Hull, who lost his sight in 1983, says that blind people always need one hand free in order to exercise their sense of touch:

> If I have to carry a cup of tea from this room into the next, I can do it. If you put a full glass into my other hand, then I cannot do it. Giving me a full glass in my second hand is like blindfolding me. . . . As long as the blind person has one free hand, he sees with that hand. He does not experience not knowing where to go or where he is so long as he can guide himself with his free hand.[17]

Simple tasks such as grocery shopping are far more complicated for the visually impaired. Each day, the blind face challenges in life.

Facing Daily Struggles

Even with so many techniques and tips, there is no question that blind people face daily struggles in their lives. Henry Grunwald, a former editor of *Time* magazine who lost most of his vision to age-related macular degeneration, finds his handicap to be a continual source of frustration. He is able to negotiate streets without a white cane, but often finds himself helpless when he arrives at his destination—unable to

read signs or fooled by what he thinks he is seeing. Grunwald
explains:

> Shopping or window-shopping is difficult. I often find it
> impossible to tell a camera from a tape recorder from a
> radio. A shop window full of shoes can look like a candy
> store and a cleaner can look like a deli. I have walked into
> a ladies' room thinking it was the men's room because I
> could not decipher the letters or the often quaint symbols
> for male and female on the door.[18]

Grunwald says he mostly misses being able to read books
and newspapers. Now he listens to audio versions of books
and periodicals or asks his wife or others to read to him. "Being read to at length is still strange," he says. "I have not had
the experience since childhood. It often makes me feel helpless and passive. Occasionally, my mind wanders."[19]

Many blind people find that their sighted friends and family
members and even strangers are very considerate and willing
to help out. And yet they also believe their struggles are often
exacerbated by sighted people, who may be well intentioned
but tend to act awkwardly around the blind. According to
Hull:

> How strange it is for sighted people to recognize that
> there is a human being who is using a stick as an exten-
> sion of his perception! It is not easy for sighted people to
> realize the implications of the fact that the blind person's
> perception of the world, sound apart, is confined to the
> reach of his body, and to any extension of his body which
> he can set up, such as a cane. This is illustrated, I think,
> by the great difficulty which most sighted people have
> in helping a lost blind person to reorientate himself. The
> indication of place which sighted people provide are usu-
> ally too general, or they presuppose that the blind person
> has a greater knowledge of his environment than he may
> actually have.[20]

Mr. Magoo: An Unfair Stereotype

From the moment he first appeared on movie screens in 1949, the animated character Mr. Magoo has generated hostility among blind people, who believe the bumbling character represents an unfair stereotype and promotes insensitivity to their plight. The vision-impaired Magoo stumbles through life, comically misusing common household objects, such as mistaking a banana for a telephone receiver. In 1997 the character was adapted to a live-action film released by the Walt Disney Company.

Activists for the blind complained about the film. Marc Maurer, an attorney and former president of the National Federation of the Blind, recalled a troubling incident that occurred when he was a nineteen-year-old freshman at the University of Notre Dame in South Bend, Indiana. Maurer says:

> I could not find a single student or professor who understood what I knew—that blind people have the capacity and can compete equally. I believed that my enrollment at Notre Dame that fall was undeniable proof of my ability. Still, as I walked the campus for the first time, I heard the words echo from a group of giggling students behind me: "Look at Mr. Magoo."

Some three thousand National Federation of the Blind members petitioned the Disney studio to shelve the film before its release. The studio declined and released the movie. *Mr. Magoo* went on to post lackluster earnings at the box office.

Marc Maurer, "There's Nothing Funny About Mr. Magoo," *Buffalo News*, August 24, 1997, p. H-5.

Prejudice Against the Blind

Sometimes, though, blind people find that sighted people are not well intentioned. Even though the Americans with Disabilities Act prohibits discrimination against blind people and others with handicaps, many blind people suspect that prospective employers are not willing to hire people with vision impairments. "The biggest barrier to employment of blind professionals is the stereotypical thinking and fears of sighted people,"[21] says Amy Ruelle, a social worker in Brockton, Massachusetts.

Blind airline reservation clerk James Gurecki uses the latest technology to help customers make travel plans.

Ruelle is severely vision impaired but not totally blind. She found her job as a counselor for mentally ill clients after an employment search that took eleven months. She sent out dozens of résumés and participated in some fifty employment interviews before landing her job. Ruelle suspects that she would have had a far easier time finding a job if she had not been visually impaired. "I certainly faced a lot of discrimination,"[22] she says.

One blind person who believes his disability has prevented him from finding employment is Albert P. Griffith, a Romulus, Michigan, man who lost his vision during infancy. Also trained as a social worker, Griffith has been unable to find work, even though he has sent out more than 250 résumés and has participated in more than one hundred employment interviews.

According to Griffith, interviewers always treat him politely but never give him reasons for turning down his applications for the jobs. Most promise to keep his résumé on file, he says. "It's called the circular file"[23]—meaning the trash can—he quickly jokes.

Under the Americans with Disabilities Act, employers are prohibited from turning down job applicants because they are disabled. Also, employers must make "reasonable" accommodations for disabled people in the workplace—such as providing wheelchair-bound workers with bathrooms that are handicapped accessible or permitting blind people to bring their guide dogs into the workplace.

Charles S. Hodge, an attorney with the U.S. Labor Department's Civil Rights Division, which enforces the Americans with Disabilities Act in the workplace, says the difficulties encountered by Griffith and Ruelle are common. "Employers have this stereotype that you must be helpless, pitiable and virtually nonfunctional if you are blind,"[24] he says.

Impediments to Travel

The workplace is not the only segment of society where blind people believe they have encountered prejudice. Blind people often find alleged cases of prejudice when they try to engage in normal, everyday activities such as shopping or traveling.

For example, in 2006 the National Federation of the Blind (NFB) sued the retail chain Target because the company did not include provisions on its Web site that would enable the visually impaired to hear audio descriptions of merchandise. In the case, a judge made an early ruling siding with the NFB and refused Target's request to dismiss the lawsuit. Brian Blair, a Florida attorney who represents businesses accused of discriminatory practices, says, "For any business that has a physical location and a website, (the ruling) says you need to take reasonable steps to permit accessibility for the disabled."[25]

As for impediments to their travel, blind people have charged that U.S. airlines sometimes engage in discriminatory practices. During the 1980s the NFB filed a complaint with the U.S. Transportation Department after two blind airline passengers were arrested for insisting on keeping their white canes with them on an airplane, instead of stowing them in overhead compartments, which had been requested by the flight crew. Other blind people claimed to have had similar encounters with airlines. For example, some blind people who took seats next to emergency exits were forced by the flight crews to sit elsewhere on the planes; the crews feared they would be in the way if the passengers were forced to make quick exits from the planes. Also, blind people objected because they were ordered to preboard planes—to take their seats before the other passengers—so they would not be in the way in the narrow aisles of the planes when the rest of the passengers board. To a blind person who seeks only to be treated equally, being forced to preboard a plane can be a belittling experience. It can also be belittling to be told they may be in the way during emergencies and therefore have to move to new seats.

Activists for the blind lobbied the federal government for antidiscrimination laws that applied to air travel. Finally,

Mainstreaming Blind Students

Although many schools for the blind continue to accept students, today most blind students, as well as other disabled students, are "mainstreamed," meaning they take classes in public schools alongside other students. Most school districts provide additional training for disabled students in so-called special education classes; nevertheless, in many public schools blind students can be found negotiating the halls between classes, eating their meals in school cafeterias, attending pep rallies, and otherwise taking part in a variety of school activities.

At the Sooke School District near Victoria, British Columbia, some 13 percent of the district's 8,250 students are disabled. Some of those disabled students are blind, including senior Kaitlyn Kerr.

As a younger student, Kerr did attend a school for the blind but later transferred to a public high school. She has found the experience of being mainstreamed challenging—such as walking through her busy high school hallways between classes. "Sometimes I walk with friends, because people get out of two people's way better than they get out of one," she says. Kerr is happy to have gone to a public school with her sighted friends. "Education-wise, I do really well, but there's always the whole thing about being different than the others," she says. "That really doesn't bother me, though, because I have a lot of friends at school."

Quoted in Jeff Bell, "Kaitlyn's Blind, and Excelling in School," *Victoria Times Colonist*, October 29, 2007. http://199.71.40.129/victoriatimescolonist/news/capital_van_isl/story.html?id=16f71a4c-2b8b-4d45-8d04-3776273d5611&k=55982.

in 1990, Congress enacted the U.S. Air Carrier Access Act, which makes it a crime for airlines to require blind people, or any other disabled persons, to sit in particular seats. Also, under the act blind people are permitted to keep their canes with them at their seats or, if they are traveling with guide dogs, for the animals to sit in the aisles of the planes. In addition, disabled people are not required to preboard planes, unless they request to do so. Finally, the act ordered aircraft manufacturers to design more handicapped-accessible features into the planes, such as seats with removable armrests that make it easier for blind people to slide in and out of the seats.

Enduring Their Blindness

Most blind people simply want to be given the chance to make a living, take advantage of the rights available to all Americans, and be treated with dignity. John Milton once said, "It is not so sad to be blind as not to be able to endure blindness."[26] For the most part, blind people have been able to come to terms with their disability. They have accepted that they are different from others and must find ways to compensate for their lack of vision. Certainly, many blind people have learned to endure their blindness and find ways to work through the daily tribulations of their handicaps and excel in what they do.

In fact, society is full of bright, energetic, and resourceful blind people who have found ways to compete on a high level alongside sighted people. For example, in Bridgewater, Massachusetts, freshman Morgayne Mulkern has won a place on her high school's cross-country team, even though she is blind. Morgayne is led through the course of city streets, rural roads, and forested paths by another runner, but Morgayne sets the pace and crosses the finish line before her guide. "She basically runs with me and tells me where there are things," Morgayne says about her guide, basketball player Ashley DeAndrade. "She'll say, 'OK, there's a hill coming up,' and 'We have to sprint at the end of the race'—little things like that so I'll know."[27]

Meanwhile, in suburban Detroit, Michigan, blind seventh-grader Jeff Humphreys won a scholarship to attend Space Camp and now dreams of becoming an astronaut or astronomer and one day taking part in a colony on the Moon. "We'll probably be discovering alien life," he says. "I think I'd like to be part of that."[28] And at the University of California, Los Angeles, student Deepa Goraya, born three months prematurely with retinopathy of prematurity, hopes to attend law school after she obtains her undergraduate degree. "Blindness is just a characteristic, not a disability," says Goraya. "It's just a mere inconvenience, and it doesn't define who I am."[29]

CHAPTER FOUR

Maintaining Healthy Eyes

In many cases eye diseases that lead to blindness are age related, meaning that most people will not suffer damage to their eyes until they reach their forties, fifties, or sixties. In fact, eye disease is regarded as one of the major health threats facing baby boomers—people who were born between 1945 and 1965. Baby boomers are regarded most at risk to develop eye disease.

For example, as people grow older they often suffer from high blood pressure, which is also known as hypertension. High blood pressure occurs when the heart has to pump harder to circulate blood through the arteries, which can narrow due to age or other medical conditions. The condition can lead to heart disease, stroke, and failure of the kidneys and other organs. It can also lead to blindness. Hypertension can damage the tiny arteries in the retina, which can develop blockages or leak blood and fluid. Eventually the optic nerves can be damaged. This condition is known as hypertensive retinopathy; as the name suggests, it afflicts people who suffer from high blood pressure.

Fortunately, people with hypertension can take steps to reduce their blood pressure. By losing weight, exercising, and changing their diets, many people can reduce their blood pressure. Also, many medications are effective in reducing hypertension.

Most teenagers and other young people do not suffer from high blood pressure as well as other conditions that could lead to vision loss. But just because young people are decades away from facing debilitating eye diseases does not mean they cannot take steps now to ensure the health of their eyes. Doctors believe that proper nutrition and other good health habits—such as refraining from smoking and alcohol use—can pay off years from now by ensuring that eyes remain healthy.

Examining the Eyes

Physicians agree that an effective way to avoid eye disease is to undergo regular vision examinations so that early problems can be identified and addressed before they develop into serious diseases. Years ago an eye test involved little more than reading the letters of the alphabet on an eye chart posted across the room, but today the tests are far more sophisticated. The doctor will use a variety of techniques and instruments to test how well the patient can see, both at a distance and up close. Also tested will be peripheral vision, depth perception, and color vision.

A young boy is given a sophisticated eye exam. Children's vision should be monitored.

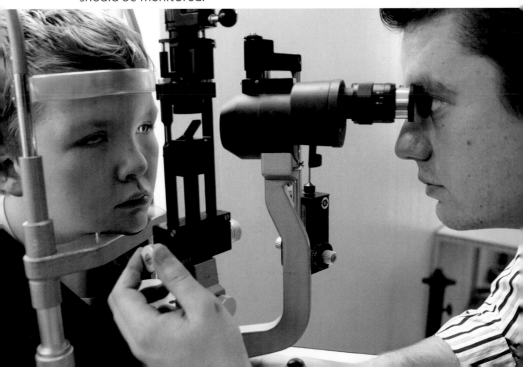

If the doctor concludes that the patient needs glasses, a re-fraction test will be performed. The patient will look through an instrument known as a Phoroptor, where he or she will see an object—often a simulated eye chart. An assortment of lenses will be flipped down in front of the eyes until the pa-tient signals that everything is in the sharpest focus possible. By inserting an artificial lens between the image and the eye's natural lens, the doctor can bend the light before the natural lens focuses it onto the retina. That is how a pair of glasses corrects faulty vision.

The doctor may also shine a light directly into the pupils to see how they react to light—they should close to block bright lights and open when the light is dim, enabling the person to see in low light.

During the examination, the doctor may make a visual in-spection of the corneas and irises, examining them for defects. The doctor may also use magnifiers to look more closely into the patient's eyes, searching for tiny scratches, scrapes, tears, infections, or other warning signs. To examine the retina, the doctor will employ eye drops that force the pupils to dilate, or open wide, so that he or she may have a clear look at the surface of the retina.

Also, the doctor may conduct a test of the retina using a dye that is injected into the patient's bloodstream. The procedure, known as a fluorescein angiography, involves the use of a cam-era to photograph the blood vessels in the retina and choroid. The dye causes the blood vessels in the retina and choroid to turn yellow, which helps the doctor tell whether they are leak-ing. The test can be used to diagnose wet age-related macular degeneration as well as diabetic retinopathy.

Another examination of the eye is the perimetry test, which requires a patient to peer into an instrument, focusing his or her eyes on a screen that displays flashes of light on different sections of the screen. Every time the light flashes, the patient pushes a button, acknowledging that he or she has seen the flash. If the patient fails to see a flash of light, the physician knows that there is a part of the screen that is not visible to

When to Get an Eye Test

A young person with healthy eyes does not need to see an eye doctor for regular tests. According to the American Academy of Ophthalmology, people who are between the ages of five and thirty-nine need only get a vision test if they suspect they have developed problems with their eyesight, such as fuzzy vision, or for more serious issues, including pain, flashes of light, or if they sustain injuries to their eyes.

Many employers require new workers to undergo eye tests, particularly if they are expected to drive cars or operate heavy machinery as part of their duties. If a doctor detects vision problems, the new employee may be asked to obtain glasses before starting work.

Children under the age of five should be screened for common eye problems, such as nearsightedness, farsightedness, crossed eyes, and lazy eye—a condition in which one eye works harder than the other. In addition, the academy recommends that adults between the ages of forty and sixty-five undergo eye examinations every two to four years, and that people over the age of sixty-five receive eye exams every one or two years. Others who are at high risk to develop eye disease, such as diabetics and people with a family history of eye disease, are urged to undergo annual vision examinations.

the patient. For example, the patient who misses flashes of light in the center of the screen may be developing AMD or glaucoma.

One of the simplest tests for glaucoma takes just a few seconds—a puff of air is shot into the eye to see how the cornea responds to pressure from the outside. If the cornea does not bend with the puff of air, it could mean there is too much pressure against the cornea on the other side—an indication that the eye may be afflicted with glaucoma.

Selecting Sunglasses

Patients who walk out of the physician's office with 20/20 vision and clean bills of eye health may find themselves squinting as they open the door into bright sunlight. They should have put on a pair of sunglasses before exposing their eyes to the harmful rays of the sun.

Sunlight contains ultraviolet (UV) radiation. Overexposure to ultraviolet radiation causes sunburns, which damage the skin. Indeed, consistent overexposure to the sun could eventually lead to skin cancer. The same radiation that damages skin causes harm to the eyes, causing cataracts and AMD. In fact, the condition known as ultraviolet keratitis—also known as snow blindness—is essentially a sunburn on the cornea. It is a very painful affliction caused by overexposure to bright lights, either directly or through glare caused by reflected sunlight off of snow or bodies of water. "Anytime you're in the outdoors, especially around snow, water or rocks, there's going to be lots of glare and reflection," says Brad Ludden, a champion whitewater kayaker. "Since I spend 90 percent of my life outdoors, I'm at risk for eye problems such as establishing cataracts early on. That's why I wear sunglasses whenever I can."[30]

Moreover, the effect on the eyes is cumulative. In 1988 a study published in the *New England Journal of Medicine* reported on the cases of 838 men who worked outdoors on the Chesapeake Bay in Maryland. The study found that the men who spent the most time outside developed cataracts at triple the rate of those who spent little time under the sun. That is why people who spend a lot of time outdoors should wear sunglasses that block at least 99 percent of the sun's ultraviolet radiation. UV-blocking sunglasses are expensive, but eye care experts say the extra cost is worth it. According to experts, when buying sunglasses people should avoid cheap pairs that sell for ten dollars or less in drug stores or department stores. And vision experts say people should avoid sunglasses sold on tables at flea markets or on street corners. Typically, these glasses are cheap knockoffs of expensive brands. Chances are, they will provide little, if any, protection against UV rays.

In fact, sunglasses that do not provide UV protection may cause more harm than good. When tinted glasses are worn over the eyes, the pupil opens to let in more light. If the glasses do not provide UV protection, it means the eye is actually letting in more harmful UV rays.

Just because the lenses are very dark does not mean they provide the maximum in UV protection. In sunglasses, the UV protection comes from a coating on the lens, not the color of the lens. In addition, even lenses that provide 100 percent UV protection will not shield the eyes against sunlight if they do not cover the entire surface of the eyes. That is why eye care experts urge people to wear wraparound sunglasses to prevent sunlight from leaking in through the sides.

In recent years contact lenses have been manufactured to provide UV protection, but since they do not cover the entire eye, experts question their value. New Jersey ophthalmologist Cary Silverman explains, "Sunglasses provide one of the best sources of UV protection. While some UV-absorbing contact lenses are now available, they do not provide adequate protection and should not replace sunglasses. Sunglasses are still needed to cover the entire eye area, including eyelids."[31]

A good pair of sunglasses usually costs at least thirty dollars. The amount of UV protection provided by the lenses will be stated on stickers affixed directly to the lenses. People who engage in active lifestyles—such as kayakers, surfers, hikers, or snowboarders—may want to invest in shatterproof lenses. Also, some people may prefer polarizing lenses, which reduce glare.

Healthy Eyes Through a Healthy Diet

Receiving regular eye examinations and protecting the eyes from sunlight are important steps to take, but there is much more that people should be doing to safeguard their vision. One important way people can help protect their eyesight is

A healthy diet can mean healthy eyes. Nutritious, lean meals lead to fewer health problems overall in later life.

by eating nutritious and fat-free meals. Indeed, perhaps one of the greatest health risks facing Americans today is obesity. According to a 2004 study by the U.S. Centers for Disease Control and Prevention, a third of all American adults and 17 percent of young people between the ages of twelve and nineteen are obese.

People who are obese face many health issues—heart disease and stroke are among their biggest concerns—but there are many other ways in which obesity can affect a person's life. Many people who are obese develop diabetes, which is caused by an overabundance of blood sugar in the body. Diabetes can damage the retinas and lead to diabetic retinopathy and blindness. In fact, a 1989 study by the Massachusetts Eye and Ear Infirmary concluded that a high-fat diet can double a person's risk of going blind late in life.

Therefore, people can reduce their risk of eye disease by eating a nutritious diet. Studies have shown that certain foods can help protect eyesight. For example, diets rich in vitamins C and E can help protect eyes against age-related macular degeneration (AMD). These vitamins are regarded as antioxidants, which help maintain healthy cells, including the cells found in the eyes. Overexposure to sunlight prompts the body to produce what are known as free radicals, which are rogue oxygen molecules. Cells in the eyes are often damaged by too much oxygen. It makes the proteins in the eye tissue sticky, which can cloud the lens and cause cataracts. An overabundance of oxygen in eye cells is also believed to cause AMD and glaucoma. The antioxidants supplied by vitamins C and E help reduce the number of free radicals in the body. "Nothing is clearer in the medical literature than the benefit of antioxidants for eye health," says Fred Pescatore, a New York City physician. "They literally undo the cellular damage caused by the sun. Antioxidants reduce these free radicals before they can cause too much damage."[32]

Foods rich in vitamin C include green and red peppers, broccoli, spinach, tomatoes, potatoes, strawberries, oranges, grapefruits, and other citrus fruits. Foods containing vitamin E include vegetable oils as well as wheat germ and nuts. Also, foods containing the vegetable pigment known as beta-carotene are effective antioxidants. These foods include carrots, winter squash, sweet potatoes, broccoli, bell peppers, tomatoes, papayas, mangoes, apricots, and watermelon. Other foods rich in antioxidants are blueberries, pomegranates, grapes, walnuts, and sunflower seeds.

The antioxidants lutein and zeaxanthin have also been found to help people maintain healthy macula cells. Both of these antioxidants are found in dark green leafy vegetables such as spinach, kale, collard greens, mustard greens, watercress, and parsley.

Ophthalmologists, Optometrists, and Opticians

Three types of professionals—ophthalmologists, optom-etrists, and opticians—are associated with eye health. Each professional performs a specific function. Depending on the seriousness of an eye ailment, it may be necessary to see all three.

An ophthalmologist is a medical doctor who special-izes in eye care. The physician has graduated from medical school and received additional training in diagnosing and treating eye diseases. Ophthalmologists can perform eye examinations, diagnose eye illnesses, prescribe medications, and perform routine eye surgeries. More complicated pro-cedures may be performed by physicians who specialize in eye surgery.

Optometrists can also perform eye examinations. Most specialize in administering refraction tests, which deter-mine how to correct poor eyesight through prescription eyeglasses. Optometrists attend schools that award doctor of optometry degrees. Many optometrists will treat minor eye ailments, but they refer more serious cases to ophthal-mologists.

Opticians are professionals who specialize in filling pre-scriptions for eyeglasses, just as pharmacists fill prescriptions for medications. Opticians will ensure that the eyeglasses contain the correct lenses and that they fit comfortably on the patient. Opticians receive specialized training in their craft, and many states require that they obtain licenses be-fore taking up the practice.

Finally, the retina contains high concentrations of zinc. Therefore, people who lack zinc in their diets may face retinal disease. Zinc can be found in most fruits and vegetables.

Smoking, Drinking, and Exercise

Overeating is just one bad habit that can lead to eye disease. Smoking and drinking can also have adverse impacts on eyesight. In 2003 a University of Wisconsin study determined that smoking and drinking enhance the production of free radicals and contribute to AMD. Moreover, it has been well established that cigarette smoke contains numerous harmful chemicals that can destroy cells and cause many harmful effects on the body, such as lung cancer. These chemicals affect not only the lungs and other organs but also the very sensitive blood vessels in the eyes. According to Robert Cykiert, a professor of ophthalmology at the New York University School of Medicine, "There are dozens of toxic chemicals in cigarette smoke that can damage blood vessels in the retina, contribute to age-related macular degeneration and cause cataracts to progress."[33]

Likewise, alcohol abuse can damage many vital organs, such as the liver. In addition, heavy drinkers have been found to be at high risk to develop cataracts. It is believed that alcohol damages the proteins that compose the tissue of the lens, blocking the absorption of nutrients that are necessary for a healthy lens. As a result, cataracts may form on the lens.

Another bad habit that can affect eyesight is failing to get enough exercise—certainly, a common trait among people who are overweight or heavy drinkers or smokers. A 2003 study published in the medical journal *Archives of Ophthalmology* found that AMD develops twice as fast in obese people as it does in people who are not overweight. Meanwhile, people who exercise at least three times a week slowed the onset of AMD by 25 percent. It is believed that inflamed blood vessels may speed the development of AMD. Since exercise helps reduce the inflammation in blood vessels, people who exercise a lot are less prone to develop AMD. A separate 2003 study published in the medical journal *American Family Physician* reported similar results for glaucoma patients—those who maintained regular exercise programs developed the disease at levels lower than people who did not exercise, probably because exercise helps reduce the inflammation of the optic nerve.

Sports and Eye Injuries

People can also maintain healthy eyesight by taking steps to prevent accidents from harming their eyes. When working around power tools, eye protection is important—sawdust, wood chips, metal shavings, and other projectiles can fly out from saws, sanders, routers, drills, and other equipment, endangering eyes. Others who routinely wear protection for their eyes are hunters, target shooters, and paintball players—participants in sports that feature projectiles.

For those players as well as participants in many team sports, trainers recommend protective eyewear made out of polycarbonate, which is twenty times stronger than the plastics used to fashion the lenses of ordinary eyeglasses. (The eyeglass industry started switching from glass lenses to plastic lenses in the 1960s.)

On a youth level, many baseball, football, and hockey leagues require players to wear eye protection. Despite those precautions, some forty thousand young athletes a year suffer injuries to their eyes during practices or games. "Sports represent the number one cause of eye injuries in children under the age of sixteen," says M. Bowes Hamill, associate professor of ophthalmology at Baylor College of Medicine in Texas. "Injuries range from abrasions of the cornea and bruised eyelids to internal eye damage, such as retinal detachments and internal bleeding. Many of these injuries lead to vision loss and permanent blindness."[34]

On a professional level, the leagues often leave the matter of eye protection to the discretion of the players. Some professional football players wear eye protection, usually polycarbonate shields across the openings of their helmets. Hockey goalies routinely wear eye protection. In fact, the masks worn

A young woman wears polycarbonate athletic glasses during her basketball game.

by goalies evolved into the so-called bird cage design following a career-ending injury in 1979 to Philadelphia Flyers goalie Bernie Parent, who was struck in the eye by a hockey stick despite wearing a form-fitting mask on his face. As a result of the injury, Parent temporarily lost vision in one eye.

Other than the catchers, few baseball players protect their eyes even though, on a Major League level, the ball often races toward the batter at speeds of 90 miles (144k) per hour or more. Indeed, most baseball players seem to have forgotten the sad story of Tony Conigliaro, the young Boston Red Sox slugger who, with a Hall of Fame future ahead of him, was struck in the face by a pitched ball during a game in 1967. Sportswriter Dick Dew recalls covering the game and seeing the pitch strike Conigliaro. "It stopped everybody in the place because of the sound of it," Dew says. "It was unmistakable. You knew the injury was serious the moment you heard it."[35]

The ball smashed Conigliaro's cheekbone and blurred his vision. After missing more than a year, Conigliaro returned to the Red Sox lineup in 1969. He managed to put together a couple

Boston Red Sox players surround teammate Tony Conigliaro after he was severely injured by a baseball. Inset is a close-up of Conigliaro's battered face.

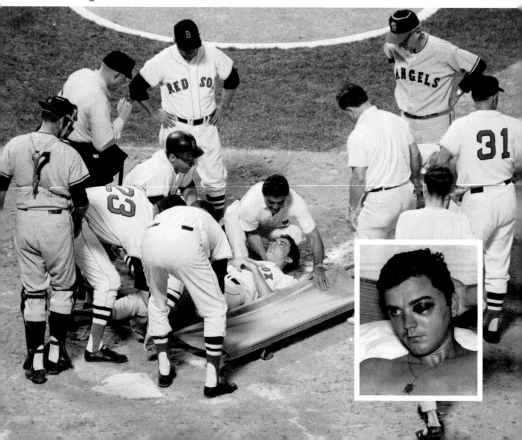

of good seasons but was eventually forced to retire because of consistent problems with his vision. Following his injury, Conigliaro was never the same player.

Symptoms Should Not Be Ignored

There is no question that athletes can avoid eye injuries by wearing protective goggles or shields over their eyes. By taking simple precautions, other people should be able to avoid eye injuries and disease as well. Indeed, one of the most tragic outcomes of debilitating eye disease in older people is that their afflictions often lead to other ills. Adults who were productive and active workers suddenly find themselves unable to function. They may become isolated from their friends or family members, which can lead to depression. Or, if they have not mastered the techniques of walking with a white cane or guide dog, they can injure themselves, perhaps breaking a hip, which can leave them bedridden. "Blindness and low vision can lead to loss of independence and reduced quality of life," says Elias A. Zerhouni, director of the National Institutes of Health. "As our population lives longer, eye disease will be an even greater concern."[36]

For many people, that sad outcome can be avoided. Vision experts urge people to learn the warning signs of eye diseases. If they notice they have difficulty reading or making out objects at a distance, they should not ignore the condition and see an eye doctor for a vision test. The problem may simply be that they need glasses. Or there may be a much more serious cause that can be discovered and addressed before it advances to a debilitating disease that can lead to permanent blindness.

CHAPTER FIVE

What Is the Future for Blind People?

There have been numerous medical advancements developed in recent years that scientists and physicians believe could help many blind people see again. Some of these advancements involve new surgical techniques, but others rest on the promises of stem cell research and the development of tiny high-tech devices that can be implanted in the eyes.

One of the most promising innovations is under development at the Doheny Eye Institute of the University of Southern California, where scientists are experimenting with a tiny device inserted into the back of the eye. Known as the Argus II, the implant receives images from a special pair of eyeglasses equipped with video cameras. The device then stimulates nerves in the eye, which accept the images transmitted by the eyeglasses.

On an experimental basis, the Argus II has been implanted in a handful of blind people, including Terry Byland, a fifty-eight-year-old Corona, California, man who has been blind for thirteen years. Byland says the implants have not given him clear vision, but he is able to see a lot more than he did prior to receiving the devices. "I can't recognize faces but I can see them like a dark shadow," he says. "I can cross a busy street—I can see white lines on the crosswalk." Byland was also able to see his eighteen-year-old son for the first time since the boy was five years old. "I don't mind saying, there were a few tears wept that day,"[37] Byland said.

By no means does Byland now enjoy clear, normal vision. Still, for someone who has lived in darkness for thirteen years, just seeing vague shapes is an enormous improvement. Certainly, if the Argus II is perfected, it could provide new hope for thousands, if not millions, of blind people.

Nevertheless, it could take years or even decades for the device to be made available to blind people—if, in fact, the Argus II is finally perfected and permitted to go into widespread use. In the United States, the Food and Drug Administration typically requires years of testing before new drugs or medical devices are approved for widespread use because many ill effects from new therapies do not always make themselves immediately apparent.

While blind people wait for the magic bullet—the drug or device that will restore their sight—new technologies are under development that could help many people with severe vision problems navigate streets, pick products from grocery store shelves, or find clothes in their closets. Certainly, these gadgets will never replace a healthy pair of eyes, but some of them may come close.

Offering Hope Through Implant Surgery

The Argus II is the not the first implant that has been employed in the effort to repair damaged eyes. Since the 1980s eye surgeons have been experimenting with enhancing the performance of retinas damaged by age-related macular degeneration (AMD) and retinitis pigmentosa by inserting artificial implants. The implants electronically stimulate the remaining healthy cells in the retina, enabling them to capture visual signals. Unlike the Argus II, these implants work without cameras transmitting signals; instead, they transmit light that enters the eye directly through the pupil.

One recipient of the implants is Paul Ladis, a Roselle, Illinois, man who lost his sight to retinitis pigmentosa in 1988. Prior to

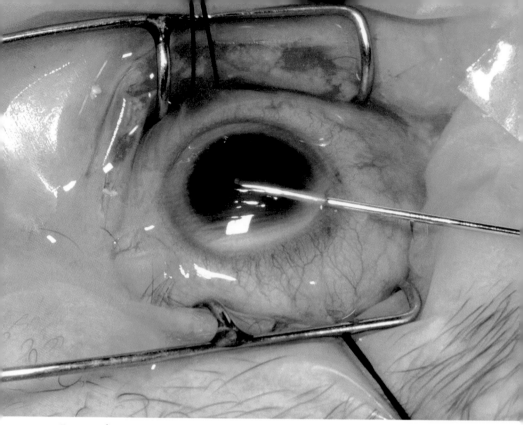

Eye implant surgery, shown here, is still in the experimental stages, but may be the wave of the future for vision restoration.

receiving the implants, Ladis could see nothing. Now Ladis can make out shapes, sources of light, and motion. Certainly, his normal vision has not been restored, but Ladis can nevertheless perform a lot more functions on his own than he could before undergoing the implant surgery. "If I want to reach out and hug my kids, I can see them walking by me now,"[38] Ladis says.

Ladis's implant contains some five thousand tiny solar cells that convert light into electrical impulses, much the same way a solar energy panel that sits atop a house converts sunlight into electricity. The energy produced by the optical implant is used to stimulate the cells in the retina.

The procedure is still experimental and has been performed on few human patients; nevertheless, results are promising and research continues. A number of private biomedical companies have invested heavily in the technology, and executives of those companies are confident the procedure will one day enter the mainstream of medical science and return vision to blind people. "The concept is no longer laughable," says Gerald Chader, chief scientist for the advocacy group Foundation Fighting Blindness. "There are patients living with implants that seem to work."[39]

A different form of implant surgery holds promise for AMD patients. People afflicted with the disease often lose their ability to read because of the foggy haze that forms in the center of their vision. To compensate, AMD patients must often read books, magazines, newspapers, and other printed materials off computer and television screens that blow up the text into huge letters.

Blind Birdwatchers

While it would seem that a birdwatcher—also known as a birder—needs a healthy pair of eyes, that is not necessarily true. More and more blind people are taking up birding, but instead of using binoculars and cameras they venture into the forests armed with sophisticated microphones and audio recording devices.

Most species of birds can be identified by their distinctive chirps. By aiming sensitive microphones at habitats, blind birdwatchers find they can identify many different types of birds. "Blind birders probably do this more instinctively than sighted birders do, and can hear birds at various distances," says John Fitzpatrick, director of the Cornell Laboratory of Ornithology in Ithaca, New York. "They're perceiving auditorily a bigger dimension to the landscape than we do when we're watching."

One blind birder, John Neville of Salt Spring Island, British Columbia, has produced five audio CDs of bird sounds. "I try to include a little bit of the language of the birds," Neville explains. "As well as the pleasure, from our perspective, of hearing the songs and being able to identify them, I try to get a little bit of the meaning of what the birds are telling each other."

Quoted in Tina Kelley, "A Sight for Sensitive Ears," *Audubon Magazine*, January 2002. http://audubonmagazine.org/birds/birds0201.html.

Some AMD patients wear large magnifying devices over their eyes. A new implant technology is designed to place those magnifiers inside the eyes. A California company, VisionCare, is developing what it calls an implantable miniature telescope (IMT), which is a tiny magnifying device, about the size of a pea, that can be inserted into the eye. The IMT magnifies an image seen by the eye, just as a telescope magnifies the image of a far-off planet or star. "For an 80-year-old to sit and watch TV or read headlines in a newspaper or pay the bills, it's a godsend,"[40] says Robert Kershner, a Tucson, Arizona, ophthalmologist who has assisted in the development of the IMT.

The Promise of Stem Cell Research

Another procedure that remains experimental is the actual transplantation of retinal tissue. So far, the procedure has been attempted on laboratory mice only. At University College London in Great Britain, scientists have taken healthy rod and cone cells from mice and have successfully transplanted them into the retinas of blind mice, partially restoring their sight.

This procedure is promising, but many roadblocks remain before it can be tried on humans. In the British experiment, the rod and cone cells were extracted from the eyes of newborn mice and then were allowed to grow and mature in the eyes of the blind mice. In humans, such transplants would be rare because the donors would have to be recently deceased persons—taking the rod and cone cells from living donors would seriously damage the eyes of the donors. Since relatively few human infants die, the pool of donors would be rather small. Still, research on laboratory animals continues. Indeed, the scientists conducting the experiments predict that human rod and cone cells can one day be transplanted. "We are now confident that this is the avenue to pursue to uncover ways of restoring vision to thousands who have lost their sight,"[41] says Robert MacLaren, a British eye surgeon who is the codirector of the research project.

Perhaps even more promising is research in which stem cells are injected into the eyes of blind people. Such procedures have already been performed on humans with large measures of success.

At the age of three, Michael May lost his sight when his corneas were damaged in an accident. Forty-three years later, the Davis, California, man underwent an experimental surgery in which stem cells were injected into his eyes. After two procedures, May's eyesight was restored. He describes the feeling:

> Those first few weeks were an incredible series of firsts. My first airplane flight, for instance. It was a very bumpy ride, and for 30 minutes I kept working on my computer. Then I looked out the window and I could see the ground. I was so excited I turned to the lady next to me and said, "Excuse me, I got my sight back last week after being totally blind for 43 years. Could you help me figure out what I'm seeing?" There was a big pause as she decided whether I was a lunatic or a miracle.[42]

Stem cells can be cultured to create all manner of human cells. It is believed that stem cells hold great promise for eradicating

Hundreds of human embryonic stem cells are bathed in special fluids. Cutting-edge therapy like stem cell injection offers great hope for the blind.

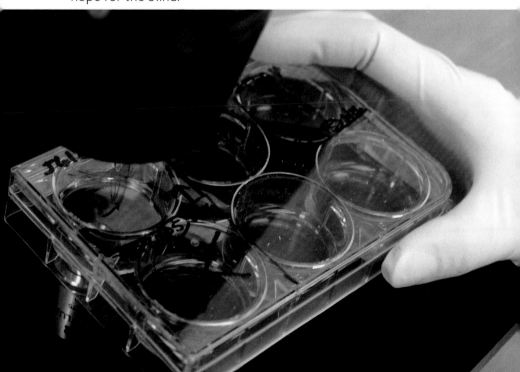

disease by replacing diseased cells with healthy cells. For example, sufferers of Parkinson's disease, a debilitating brain disease that leads to loss of motor skills, may receive relief from stem cell therapy because the new cells can be used to repair the brain damage caused by the disease. Likewise, victims of accidents that have caused damage to their spinal cords, making them incapable of using their arms and legs, believe new cells can be grown in their spinal cords, thus repairing the damage. Certainly, as May's example shows, stem cell research holds great potential for blind people as well.

Stem cells can be drawn from adult donors, but scientists believe that embryonic stem cells hold much greater promise. Embryonic stem cells are withdrawn from unborn embryos, created not through the human sexual act but at in vitro fertilization clinics, where the egg is withdrawn from the mother and fertilized outside the womb. At these clinics, unused embryos are discarded; frequently, however, couples will donate them to laboratories that pursue stem cell research.

The development of embryonic stem cell research has slowed in the United States due to intense political opposition. Conservative politicians oppose the research, arguing that embryos—even those that are just a few days old—are human lives, and that they should not be destroyed under any circumstances, even in the pursuit of medical research. For years, the U.S. government has cut off most funding for embryonic stem cell research programs, but state governments and private donors have made up some of the lost funding. Meanwhile, candidates for president in 2008 have declared their support for stem cell research, giving supporters of the therapy hope that funding channels can soon reopen.

Similar to Treating Cancer

While the debate rages over stem cell therapy, some researchers are experimenting with more traditional forms of slowing eye disease, such as the development of new drugs. In recent years researchers have found that drugs useful in battling cancer can be effective in stemming the progression of wet AMD.

One of the ways in which physicians slow the spread of cancer is to kill the rogue blood vessels that support the growth of cancerous tumors. That therapy has been tried with some success on the rogue blood vessels that form in the eyes, causing wet AMD.

These drugs are known as angiogenesis inhibitors. (*Angiogenesis* is the medical term for the growth of new blood vessels.) When used to treat patients who suffer from AMD, the drugs must be injected right into the eye. One of the recipients of angiogenesis inhibitor therapy is the actor Dabney Coleman, who has made a career of portraying tyrannical bosses. An avid tennis player, in 2000 Coleman started having trouble seeing the ball. "This is scary," he recalls. "I can't see the ball. I had no depth perception." Soon, Coleman was diagnosed with AMD. Eventually his eyesight deteriorated to 20/400—in other words, he was legally blind. In 2002 Coleman underwent the experimental drug therapy. A week after the injections, his eyesight had improved to 20/40. "No one wants a needle in the eye, but I had very little alternative,"[43] says Coleman.

Radiation therapy, which is also used routinely in cancer cases, has been applied to patients afflicted with AMD. In radiation therapy, cancerous cells are killed by exposure to X-rays. In recent years equipment has been developed that helps doctors aim the X-rays with much more precision, meaning that fewer healthy cells are killed. Armed with this technology, physicians have been able to aim X-rays at diseased cells in the macula while preserving the nearby healthy cells. So far, AMD patients who have undergone radiation therapy on their eyes have been able to maintain the same level of vision for eighteen months following the procedures.

Talking Prescription Bottles

The widespread use of electronic implants, stem cell therapy, cell transplants, angiogenesis inhibitors, and similar experimental procedures may be years or decades away from fruition.

A voice synthesizer in a "talking prescription bottle" reads drug label information out loud for this blind man.

Meanwhile, engineers have conceived many products designed to make life a bit easier for blind people. These products, which are constantly being refined and improved, are readily available to blind people.

For example, the Department of Veterans Affairs has provided compact bar code scanners to Iraq and Afghanistan veterans who suffered eye damage; the scanners enable them to employ bar codes sewn into their clothes and other possessions that respond with audible signals. In other words, when the scanner is run across a bar code sewn into a garment hanging in a closet, a prerecorded computerized voice can identify the garment as a blue sweater, a white shirt, or a gray pair of slacks.

The bar codes can also be attached to cans or boxes in the cupboard, helping the blind user tell the difference between a can of tomato soup and a can of string beans. Or, the scanner can tell the blind person that he or she has just reached for a box of cereal instead of a box of dishwasher powder.

The technology was developed by David Raistrick, a computer programmer from Chicago who produced an audible bar code scanner for an uncle who lost his vision. Originally, Raistrick pasted the bar codes onto a deck of cards because his uncle missed playing cards. Soon, Raistrick saw the potential of the scanner and adapted the bar code technology to all manner of consumer products and household items. "The device helps people find the can of beans they want to warm up and not get confused with a can of soup," says Raistrick. "Any information sighted people have from products, [the scanner] makes available to the visually impaired."[44]

Raistrick also designed a bar code scanner specifically for prescription medications. He found that blind people often struggle to figure out which pills to take—most drug containers are small with labels that include tiny lettering. Raistrick says many blind people try to take their medications by feeling the shape of the pill, which is a dangerous practice since it can be easy to mistake one pill for another. By employing the audible bar code reader, a blind person can easily identify a bottle of medication and receive other information, such as the prescribed dosage as well as the proper time of day to take the pill. Since the bar code readers were first introduced in 2000, Raistrick's company has made several improvements, including refining the voice to sound less like a robot and more like a person. "This technology is a real breakthrough for individuals who have difficulty reading their pharmacy labels,"[45] says John Fales, president of the Blinded American Veterans Association.

New Technology for White Canes

Audio technology is also being applied elsewhere to help blind people find their way around their homes and hometowns. In many cities, municipal engineers have installed audio signals at intersections that alert pedestrians when it is permissible for them to cross. In San Francisco, California, buses and commuter trains have been equipped with transmitters that

The Zebra Fish and Human Sight

The zebra fish is a tiny fish found in tropical waters. The fish gets its name from its distinctive zebralike stripes. The fish has long fascinated scientists, though, for another reason: It has the unique ability to grow new cells in its eyes, repairing diseased and damaged cells. Those cells are known as Muller glial cells, which are also present in human eyes. Unlike the zebra fish, though, the Muller glial cells in humans remain inactive.

At University College London's Institute of Ophthalmology, scientists have found a way to culture Muller glial cells, making them become active. The cells replicate themselves, and, theoretically, can replace damaged eye cells in humans. Successful experiments have been conducted on laboratory animals. In the future, scientists hope to withdraw Muller glial cells from a blind person, culture them into larger numbers and then inject them back into the patient's eyes. According to Astrid Limb, who has studied Muller glial cells, "Muller cells with stem cell properties could potentially restore sight to someone who is losing or has lost their sight due to diseased or damaged retinas. Because they are so easy to grow, we could make cell banks and have cell lines available to the general population."

Quoted in Fiona MacRae, "Could This Remarkable Little Fish Help Find a Cure for Blindness?" *London Daily Mail*, August 1, 2007, p. 1.

The tiny zebra fish can grow new eye cells. Scientists are working to harness this ability for human eye cells.

send signals to handheld devices. As the vehicle approaches, a vision-impaired rider can point the device at the bus or train and hear a message stating the vehicle's destination. The device can also be used to locate restrooms, vending machines, exits, and boarding areas.

There has also been new technology applied to the venerable old white cane. New models transmit sound waves, helping the blind person detect approaching objects: As the white cane comes near an object, the handle vibrates; the closer the white cane comes to an object, the more vigorous the vibration.

People who suffer from AMD can make use of magnifiers that can be installed over television sets or computer screens. The magnifiers enhance contrast and enlarge type. "This makes a world of difference to people with macular degeneration, since they often lose contrast very early,"[46] says Lylas Mogk, director of visual rehabilitation at the Henry Ford Health System in Detroit.

If vision-impaired people prefer not to install magnifiers on their computer screens, there is software available that magnifies the type and improves contrast without the need for extra equipment. In addition, blind people can install software on their computers that will read the text on their screens. Scanners are also available that can read the type in a book.

Engineers have now adapted global positioning system (GPS) technology to individual users. The same technology that enables automobile drivers to find their way through unfamiliar streets can now be carried on the back of a blind person. The device is about the size of a textbook and enables the user to find his or her way through unfamiliar territory. Paul Ponchillia, a university professor who lost his sight thirty years ago, used a GPS device while taking a kayaking and hiking trip through Alaska. Ponchillia says, "I was able to walk freely around and never have to worry about getting lost."[47]

Nothing the Blind Cannot Accomplish

While the advances in technology, drug therapy, and stem cell research hold great hope for many blind people, there is no question that science will not provide all the answers. The pop singer and composer Stevie Wonder, who has been blind since shortly after his birth because of retinitis pigmentosa, had hoped to undergo experimental implant surgery. After an evaluation by doctors, Wonder was turned down for the procedure. The physicians determined that Wonder's retinas had sustained too much damage from the disease, meaning the implants would not have restored his vision.

Despite the disappointment of not being a candidate for implant surgery, Wonder has never let his blindness get in the way of his life. During an entertainment career that has spanned more than four decades, Wonder has been one of the world's most successful blind people. In the 1960s, 1970s, and 1980s, he won twenty-two Grammy Awards and recorded a string of hit songs that included "Superstition," "You Are the Sunshine of My Life," and "My Cherie Amour." Now nearly sixty years old, Wonder continues to tour, playing his hits before sold-out audiences and recording new songs. And he recalls the words of his mother, who died in 2006. Aisha Morris taught her son that even without vision, there was nothing he could not accomplish—a message that most blind people take to heart. "[She] allowed me to be free," Wonder says. "She told me, 'Your being blind doesn't mean you have to be blind.'"[48]

Notes

Introduction: Who Are the Blind?

1. Quoted in *Nation's Health*, "Few Americans Aware of Eye Disease Risk, New Survey Finds," October 2007, p. 19.
2. *UN Chronicle*, "300 Million Will Have Impaired Vision in 2020," 1997, p. 80.
3. Quoted in National Federation of the Blind, "Meet the Blind." www.nfb.org/nfb/Meet_the_Blind.asp?SnID=87221941.

Chapter 1: What Causes Blindness?

4. Quoted in Bryan Keough and Shivani Vora, "Aging Population, Chronic Diseases Fuel Rise in Debilitating Cases of 'Low Vision,'" *Wall Street Journal*, August 29, 2006, p. D-1.
5. Quoted in Keough and Vora, "Aging Population, Chronic Diseases Fuel Rise in Debilitating Cases of 'Low Vision,'" p. D-1.
6. Quoted in Felicia Fonseca, "Blinded in War, North Carolina Vet, Others Set New Goals for Changed Lives," *Myrtle Beach Sun News*, October 20, 2007. www.myrtle beachonline.com/564/story/223889.html.

Chapter 2: The Long Road to Equality

7. Quoted in *NewsHour*, "A Tale for All Ages: The *Odyssey*," March 13, 1997. www.pbs.org/newshour/forum/march97/odyssey_3-13.html.
8. John Milton, "On His Blindness," in *The Oxford Book of English Verse: 1250–1900*, ed. Arthur Quiller-Couch. www.bartleby.com/101/318.html.
9. Quoted in Frances A. Koestler, *The Unseen Minority: A Social History of Blindness in the United States*. New York: David McKay, 1976, p. 397.
10. Helen Keller, *The Story of My Life*. New York: Bantam, 1990, p. 15.

11. Quoted in Bill Quinn, "Playboy Interview: Ray Charles," *Playboy*, March 1970, p. 76.
12. Quoted in Quinn, "Playboy Interview," p. 78.
13. Kenneth Jernigan, "Blindness: Is History Against Us?" National Federation of the Blind. www.blind.net/pba 1973.htm.

Chapter 3: What Is Life Like for Blind People?

14. Quoted in *San Francisco Chronicle*, "Judge: Make Money Recognizable to the Blind," November 29, 2006. www.sf gate.com/cgi-bin/article.cgi?f=/n/a/2006/11/29/national/ w063714S22.DTL.
15. John C. Ostiund, "Blind Trust," *WE Magazine*, January/February 1999, p. 102.
16. Ostiund, "Blind Trust," p. 102.
17. John M. Hull, *Touching the Rock: An Experience of Blindness*. New York: Vintage, 1992, pp. 108–109.
18. Henry Grunwald, *Twilight: Losing Sight, Gaining Insight*. New York: Alfred A. Knopf, 2000, p. 72.
19. Grunwald, *Twilight*, p. 79.
20. Hull, *Touching the Rock*, p. 37.
21. Quoted in Jeffrey A. Tannenbaum, "Blind Seek, but Don't Often Find Adequate Jobs," *Wall Street Journal*, December 26, 2000, p. B-1.
22. Quoted in Tannenbaum, "Blind Seek, but Don't Often Find Adequate Jobs," p. B-1.
23. Quoted in Tannenbaum, "Blind Seek, but Don't Often Find Adequate Jobs," p. B-1.
24. Quoted in Tannenbaum, "Blind Seek, but Don't Often Find Adequate Jobs," p. B-1.
25. Quoted in Laura Parker, "National Federation of the Blind Files Target Lawsuit," *USA Today*, October 26, 2006. www.usatoday.com/news/nation/2006-10-25-blind_x.htm.
26. Quoted in Homer B. Sprague, ed., *Milton's Paradise Lost*. Boston: Ginn, 1886, p. 170.
27. Quoted in Jim Fenton, "Being Blind Doesn't Stop Morgayne Mulkern from Running Cross-Country at B-R, with Help from Ashley DeAndrade," *Brockton Enterprise*,

October 27, 2007. http://enterprise.southofboston.com/
articles/2007/10/22/news/news/news17.txt.

28. Quoted in Kim North Shine, "Blind Warren Student
Lives Out His Dream at Space Camp," *Detroit Free
Press*, October 21, 2007. www.freep.com/apps/pbcs.dll/
article?AID=/20071021/CFP07/710210497/1110/NEWS.

29. Quoted in Brett Noble, "Blindness Not an Inhibiting Fac-
tor," *Daily Bruin*, October 15, 2007. www.dailybruin.ucla.
edu/news/2007/oct/15/emblindness-not-inhibiting-factorem.

Chapter 4: Maintaining Healthy Eyes

30. Quoted in Mark Anders, "The Eyes Have It," *Boys' Life*,
June 2006, p. 44.

31. Quoted in *American Fitness*, "Sunglass Safety," July/
August 2004, p. 24.

32. Quoted in Aviva Patz, "Sight Saviors," *Natural Health*,
October 2006, p. 57.

33. Quoted in Patz, "Sight Saviors," p. 57.

34. M. Bowes Hamill, "Protective Eyewear Prevents Injuries,"
EnVision, spring 2004. www.lighthouse.org/education-
services/professional-education/patient-management/
patient-management-sports-eye-safety.

35. Quoted in *New York Times*, "Tony Conigliaro, Ex-Outfielder,
45, Starred for Red Sox," February 26, 1990, p. D-11.

36. Quoted in *Nation's Health*, "Vision Loss an Increasing
Public Health Problem," June/July 2004, p. 14.

Chapter 5: What Is the Future for Blind People?

37. Quoted in Julie Wheldon, "Bionic Eye Could Overcome
Blindness Within Two Years," *London Daily Mail*, February 17, 2007, p. 21.

38. Quoted in Brad Stone, "Seeing Is Believing: Hope for the
Blind," *Newsweek*, May 19, 2003, p. 63.

39. Quoted in Stone, "Seeing Is Believing," p. 63.

40. Quoted in Stone, "Seeing Is Believing," p. 63.

41. Quoted in Becky McCall, "Cell Transplant May Restore
Lost Sight," *New Scientist*, November 11, 2006, p. 14.

42. Quoted in Maureen Harrington, "Learning to See," *People*,
November 24, 2003, p. 123.

43. Quoted in Richard Jerome, "Out of the Darkness," *People*, May 6, 2002, p. 155.

44. Quoted in Howard Wolinsky, "Family Raises the Bar in Helping the Blind," *Chicago Sun-Times*, September 5, 2006, p. 49.

45. Quoted in *PR Newswire*, "ScripTalk Talking Prescriptions Awarded by Veterans Group," June 19, 2002, p. 1.

46. Quoted in Deborah Kotz, "Way Beyond Glasses," *U.S. News & World Report*, March 5, 2007, p. 69.

47. Quoted in Marcelo Prince, "GPS Technology Helps Blind Find Way," *Wall Street Journal*, May 17, 2004, p. A-1.

48. Quoted in Dan DeLuca, "Stevie Wonder, Obedient Son," *Philadelphia Inquirer*, October 30, 2007, p. E-1.

Glossary

accommodation: The natural ability of the eye's lens to change shape in order to bring an image into focus.

cataract: A cloud or streak that forms on the lens, often due to aging. Cataracts cause fuzzy vision and could result in blindness, although many cases can be corrected through surgery.

cornea: A layer of clear tissue on the front of the eye; shaped like a dome, the cornea bends the light that strikes the eye, directing it onto the lens inside.

diabetic retinopathy: The deterioration of the retina in diabetics caused by blood vessels that leak because of high blood sugar content.

glaucoma: A buildup of pressure in the eye caused by a blockage that prevents the drainage of vitreous humor; the disease can cause blindness by forcing a deterioration of the optic nerve.

iris: The colorful portion of the eye that contains muscles adjusting the size of the pupil.

lens: The clear tissue that focuses the light projected on the retina at the rear of the eye.

macula: The region at the center of the retina; densely packed with cells, the macula enables a person to read and perform other close-up functions, such as working with tools or sewing.

macular degeneration: A disease that causes destruction of cells in the macula; it could develop over a period of years through the process of aging or quickly due to the leakage of rogue blood vessels that grow in the retina.

optic nerve: The bundle of nerves that transmits, through electrical impulses and chemical reactions, images collected by the retina to the brain.

pupil: The dark spot at the center of the iris; essentially a hole that opens and closes to admit light into the eye.

retina: Located at the back of the eye, the retina contains millions of cells that collect images projected by the cornea and lens and then transmits them to the brain.

retinitis pigmentosa: A disease that causes the deterioration of the cells in the retina; it causes night blindness and tunnel vision and could lead to total blindness.

sclera: The white portion of the eye, it is the tough outer surface that protects the eye.

vitreous cavity: The globelike space that gives the eye its round shape.

vitreous humor: The clear, jellylike substance that fills the vitreous cavity, keeping it from collapsing.

Organizations to Contact

American Foundation for the Blind (AFB)

11 Penn Plaza, Suite 300
New York, NY 10001
(212) 502-7600
fax: (212) 502-7777
e-mail: afbinfo@afb.net
Web site: www.afb.org

The AFB helps provide resources to blind people, including educational opportunities and career counseling. The foundation also helps blind people obtain braille books and other products. The AFB is the custodian of the books, notes, letters, and other materials of Helen Keller, which are housed at the organization's headquarters in New York. Many of Keller's letters and other documents are available in a searchable database on the AFB Web site.

Biotechnology Industry Organization (BIO)

1201 Maryland Ave. SW, Suite 900
Washington, DC 20024
(202) 962-9200
e-mail: info@bio.org
Web site: www.bio.org

The Biotechnology Industry Organization is the nation's most influential advocate for stem cell research, which many scientists believe could hold great promise for restoring lost vision. BIO represents more than five hundred American companies that serve the health-care industry, including many that are exploring stem cell research. Students can find position papers and other resources examining stem cell research on the organization's Web site.

Foundation Fighting Blindness

11435 Cronhill Dr.
Owings Mills, MD 21117-2220
(888) 394-3937
e-mail: info@blindness.org
Web site: www.blindness.org

Since its inception in 1971, the Foundation Fighting Blindness has raised more than $270 million for medical research projects that seek a cure for the diseases that cause blindness. Students who visit the organization's Web site can find numerous updates on research projects that explore cell transplants, implant technology, and other advances. Visitors can also find explanations of all the major eye diseases.

Glaucoma Research Foundation

251 Post St., Suite 600
San Francisco, CA 94108
(800) 826-6693
fax: (415) 986-3763
Web site: www.glaucoma.org

The Glaucoma Research Foundation has raised more than $45 million for medical research since the group's inception in 1978. Students can find an explanation of the disease, several statistics on glaucoma, a glossary, and news stories about glaucoma research posted on the foundation's Web site.

Macular Degeneration Foundation

PO Box 531313
Henderson, NV 89053
(888) 633-3937
fax: (702) 450-3396
Web site: www.eyesight.org

The Macular Degeneration Foundation supports medical research aimed at eradicating the disease. All copies of the organization's newsletter, the *Magnifier*, are available online; the publication reports news on advancements in macular degeneration research.

National Eye Institute (NEI)

2020 Vision Pl.
Bethesda, MD 20892-3655
(301) 496-5248
e-mail: 2020@nei.nih.gov
Web site: www.nei.nih.gov

Part of the National Institutes of Health, the National Eye Institute provides funding for research projects that aim to prevent blindness or restore vision to blind people. Each year the NEI awards about sixteen hundred grants to physicians and researchers working at some 250 universities, hospitals, and other medical institutions. Visitors to the agency's Web site can find many resources on eye disease, including statistics, photographs, charts, and other illustrations.

National Federation of the Blind (NFB)

1800 Johnson St.
Baltimore, MD 21230
(410) 659-9314
fax: (410) 685-5653
Web site: www.nfb.org

The fifty-thousand-member NFB defends the rights of blind people and lobbies for changes in laws that would allow blind people to function in society. The NFB also promotes the development of technology and consumer products that assist the blind. Visitors to the federation's Web site can download many publications that spell out the rights of blind people as well as the NFB's programs to expand those rights.

U.S. Centers for Disease Control and Prevention

Office of Communication
Building 16, D-42
1600 Clifton Rd. NE
Atlanta, GA 30333
(800) 311-3435
e-mail: cdcinfo@cdc.gov
Web site: www.cdc.gov

The federal government's chief public health agency explores trends in diseases and other conditions that affect the health of Americans. Visitors to the agency's Web site can find pages devoted to eye safety as well as obesity, which is regarded as a primary cause of diabetic retinopathy.

World Health Organization (WHO)

Avenue Appia 20
CH-1211 Geneva 27
Switzerland
phone: 41 22 791 2111
fax: 41 22 791 3111
e-mail: info@who.int
Web site: www.who.int/en

WHO is the public health arm of the United Nations. The agency has established the Prevention of Blindness program, which is designed to wipe out trachoma and other treatable diseases that threaten the eyesight of millions of people in developing nations. Students can find many resources and publications about trachoma available on the WHO Web site, including maps that show how the disease has spread in South America, Africa, and Asia.

For Further Reading

Books

Helmet Buettner, ed., *Mayo Clinic on Vision and Eye Health*. Rochester, MN: Mayo Clinic, 2002. Published by one of the nation's leading research hospitals, the book provides a comprehensive overview of all major eye diseases. The book also includes tips for maintaining good eye health and what a patient can expect during an eye examination.

Henry Grunwald, *Twilight: Losing Sight, Gaining Insight*. New York: Alfred A. Knopf, 2000. The former *Time* magazine editor tells about his journey through age-related macular degeneration and recounts the experiences of other writers who experienced vision loss, including humorist James Thurber and novelists Henry James and Aldous Huxley.

Helen Keller, *The Story of My Life*. New York: Bantam, 1990. The woman who lost her eyesight and hearing to meningitis tells the story of her education under the guidance of her teacher, Anne Sullivan. The book includes numerous letters Helen wrote as a girl and young woman, containing very vivid impressions of the people she knew as well as the world around her.

Barbara Kiefer Lewalski, *The Life of John Milton: A Critical Biography*. Hoboken, NJ: John Wiley & Sons, 2002. An extensive biography of the poet, chronicling how Milton produced some of the most important works of English literature despite losing his sight at the age of forty-four.

Andrew P. Schachat et al., *The Johns Hopkins White Papers: Vision*. Baltimore: Johns Hopkins University, 2004. Published by one of the nation's leading medical schools, the book provides an overview of eye health and eye diseases and recommends lifestyle changes such as eating a nutritious diet and giving up smoking as ways in which eye health can be enhanced.

Periodicals

Mark Anders, "The Eyes Have It!" *Boys' Life*, June 2006. This article explains the importance of outdoor vision protection in blocking harmful ultraviolet radiation and makes recommendations on how to select sunglasses.

Maureen Harrington, "Learning to See," *People*, November 24, 2003. Harrington tells the story of Michael May, who regained his sight after forty-three years of blindness. May underwent two procedures in which stem cells were implanted in his eyes.

Deborah Kotz, "Way Beyond Glasses," *U.S. News & World Report*, March 5, 2007. The article chronicles many of the advancements in technology that enable the blind to read computer screens, make their way through city traffic, and listen to books read by devices that scan the text and produce audio versions.

Michelle Meadows, "Saving Your Sight," *FDA Consumer*, March/April 2002. The article presents an overview of the major eye diseases, including age-related macular degeneration, glaucoma, cataracts, and diabetic retinopathy. The article summarizes the warning signs and treatments for the illnesses and recommends lifestyle changes that can help prevent eye disease.

Brad Stone, "Seeing Is Believing: Hope for the Blind," *Newsweek*, May 19, 2003. The story reports on some of the latest advancements in implant technology, which can artificially stimulate damaged retinas, enabling blind people to regain at least some of their vision.

Web Sites

American Masters: Ray Charles (www.pbs.org/wnet/amer icanmasters/database/charles_r.html). This is a companion Web site to the PBS documentary series *American Masters*, which included an episode on the life of Ray Charles. Born into poverty in Albany, Georgia, Charles went blind as a young boy, but by the time he was fifteen he had become an accomplished musician and singer. He later went on to become the twentieth century's most important voice in rhythm and blues.

International Guide Dog Federation (www.ifgdsb.org. uk). This British-based organization represents more than seventy groups worldwide that train guide dogs for blind people. The group's Web site includes a history of how guide dogs have been trained to assist the blind. Also, many of the member organizations have provided stories, photos, and videos of their activities that are available online.

Marla Runyan (www.marlarunyan.com). The former Olympic athlete tells her personal story of how her vision degenerated to 20/400 as a victim of a rare form of childhood macular degeneration. She still found a way to compete, becoming an active soccer player, gymnast, and track star.

NewsHour: The Odyssey (www.pbs.org/newshour/forum/march97/odyssey_3-13.html). This is a companion Web site to the PBS news series *NewsHour*, which explored the importance of the ancient Greek poem the *Odyssey;* visitors to the site can find commentary by Princeton University literature professor Robert Fagles on many of the themes in the poem, including how the poet Homer explored blindness.

Perkins School for the Blind Museum (www.perkins museum.org/museum). The Perkins School for the Blind, which was the first school for the blind established in the United States, has made an online museum available to Internet users. Visitors can read a history of the school as well as biographies of teachers, including school founder John Dix Fisher, and students Anne Sullivan and Laura Bridgman.

Index

Picture Credits

About the Author

Hal Marcovitz has written more than one hundred books for young readers. His other title in the Diseases and Disorders series is *Infectious Mononucleosis*. A former newspaper reporter, he lives in Chalfont, Pennsylvania, with his wife, Gail, and daughters, Michelle and Ashley.